The New Dow Jones-Irwin Guide to Zero Coupon Investments

The New Dow Jones-Irwin Guide to Zero Coupon Investments

Donald R. Nichols

DOW JONES-IRWIN
Homewood, Illinois 60430

Project editor: Jane Lightell
Production manager: Ann Cassady
Designer: Mark Swimmer
Compositor: Publication Services, Inc.
Typeface: 11/13 Times Roman
Printer: R. R. Donnelley & Sons

Library of Congress Cataloging-in-Publication Data
Nichols, Donald R., 1948–
    The new Dow Jones-Irwin guide to zero coupon
investments.
    Includes index.
    1. Zero coupon securities.   I. Title.
HG4651.N534 1989   332.63'232   88–35810
ISBN: 1-55623-213-6

DEDICATION

To Mark F. Schultz at the Chicago office of Shearson Lehman Hutton, who has been generous in giving me material for my books and astute in offering my clients an excellent variety of zero coupon products. If you're interested in a conscientious broker for your zeros, he can be reached at (800) 621-5231 nationally and at (800) 572-9055 within Illinois.

I also offer special thanks and appreciation to Mark Donohue of Gabriele Hueglin & Cashman in New York, an exceedingly knowledgeable broker of zeros who works for one of the best bond houses in the business. He can be reached at (800) 422-7435 nationally.

INTRODUCTION

In the early 1980s several investment bankers hit upon an idea that made investors as much money as it made for brokers. They purchased millions of dollars worth of U.S. Treasury bonds and reconfigured them into a new type of security that paid no immediate or semiannual interest.

A conventional Treasury bond is an ornate green certificate about the size of typing paper. The bond is perforated into two sections: the first represents the U.S. Treasury Department's obligation to repay the principal—the amount you loaned the Treasury when you bought the bond—and the second section is subdivided into coupons representing your entitlement to semiannual interest payments—your return for lending the government money.

For example, let's say you bought a twenty-year Treasury bond for $1,000 that paid interest of $50 every May and November. The first section of the bond declares the Treasury's obligation to pay you back your $1,000 (called *par value*) when the bond matures in 20 years, and the second half contains 40 small coupons that you may present to any bank in order to claim your $50 interest payments each May and November for 20 years.

Now imagine a stack of 100 bonds, each laid neatly atop the other. You know that in 20 years the Treasury will have to pay you $100,000 to redeem the par value of those 100 bonds ($1,000 times 100 bonds). What's more, every May and November the Treasury will have to pay you $5,000 ($50 times 100 bonds) when you present the coupons.

That's an attractive vision, but it's cumbersome. Every six months you'll have to clip all those coupons, and in 20 years you'll have to tote the bonds down to the bank to claim your repayment of principal. There's another problem: in order to receive the maximum return from your bonds, you'd have to reinvest each of those coupon payments in a savings account or money market fund. Because interest rates fluctuate, you don't really know how much money you'd have from your total investment.

The investment bankers looked at their stacks of bonds and noticed something interesting: the pile of coupons, all identical and all paying interest on the same day each May and November, resembled *one single bond*. The same was true of the half of the bonds representing entitlement to principal. All of those were, in effect, like one bond when you put them all together. When it came down to cases, the government's $5,000 interest payment every May and November was no different from repaying $5,000 worth of principal every six months.

So they asked themselves, "Why not sell all of those coupons (and maybe the principal, too) as if they were one bond?"

However, there was one consideration. Investors demand interest in return for lending money. Conventional government bonds—any bond, in fact—paid *coupon* interest to people who clipped the coupons every six months. If you resold all the coupons as one bond, how would you pay interest to lenders?

Their answer: sell the coupons and the principal as separate bonds, but sell them at a price less than their terminal value.

Investors would receive interest as the difference between what they paid and what the "bonds" were worth when they matured. Investors would make one investment, and at maturity they would receive one payment. For convenience, the investment bankers structured their "bonds" in par values of $1,000, the customary par of most bonds.

Out of this discovery came the *zero coupon bond* that paid "accreted" rather than coupon interest by "stripping" the coupon half of the bond from the par value half and selling them separately.

These now-familiar zero coupon bonds represent a bestiary of financial felines: TIGRs (Treasury Investment Growth Receipts) from Merrill Lynch, CATS (Certificates of Accrual on Treasury Securities) from Salomon Bros., and LIONs (Lehman Investment Opportunity Notes) from Lehman Brothers. There are also COUGRS and ETRs and TBRs and the Treasury Department's book-entry zeros, called STRIPS (Separate Trading of Registered Interest and Principal of Securities).

These securities are "derivative zeros" because they're derived from an existing bond. However, many corporations have issued zero coupon bonds at attractive prices and yields. Broadly traded in public markets, corporate zeros provide ready liquidity and other advantages.

Municipal bonds issued as zeros pay federally tax-free interest. Following 1986 tax reform, municipal zeros have become exceptionally attractive, particularly to investors who no longer can deduct contributions to an IRA. What's more, innovations in the municipal bond market have created new and versatile municipal products, such as the convertible zero, which functions as both a zero coupon bond and conventional coupon bond and is a superb substitute for conventional annuities.

Astute brokerage houses have assembled packages of zero coupon bonds and retailed them in target funds, tax-exempt securities trusts, and zero coupon bond funds. Indirect investment offers some exceptional opportunities over purchasing the zeros outright, including dollar cost averaging. In fact, one of the nation's most popular investment vehicles—the money market fund—is really a form of indirect investment in short-term zero coupon instruments like commercial paper, repurchase agreements, and Treasury bills.

Banks and S&Ls caught the zero craze, and they began offering zero coupon certificates of deposit, which work just like zero coupon bonds except that they're CDs.

New types of zeros are appearing almost daily in financial markets. For instance, there's a new investment program that mates zero coupon securities with commodities funds. Part of your investment goes into zeros and part is used for commodities speculation. Thanks to the predictability and security of zeros, you're guaranteed at least to break even, thereby removing downside risk while striving for upside potential from speculation in commodities.

Even though these innovative products have much investment appeal, some of the old zeros are still the best zeros. U.S. Treasury bills and other zeros with short-term maturities provide capital stability and market-level returns that are ideal for savings. EE Savings Bonds combine the features of long-term capital growth in securities that become current income investments later in their lives.

Each form of zero coupon investment—and *investment* is more accurate than *bond* because now there are many types of zeros—offers an exceptional array of advantages.

- They provide highly predictable returns. If you hold a zero coupon security until maturity, you'll receive a stated par value, nearly always $1,000, although there are exceptions.
- They come in a range of maturites. You can buy a zero maturing tomorrow morning or one maturing in the next century.
- They escape "reinvestment risk"—the uncertainty associated with having to reinvest coupon payments at unpredictable rates.
- They can provide impressive returns, especially over longer maturities.
- As you'll see, some types of zeros offer special features that fit selected investment needs, making them even more attractive once you understand their singularities.
- Zero CDs and government bonds assembled by brokerages as zeros are virtually immune to default.
- Further, zero coupon investments can be serialized to provide current income as they mature.

However, every investment has a catch, and zeros are no exception.

First, accreted interest from most zeros is usually taxable each year, even though it's not paid until maturity. If you pay $600 for a zero coupon security maturing in 10 years at $1,000, the IRS usually expects to see some portion of the $400 accreted interest declared as current income every year. This unusual situation is called "taxation on phantom interest."

Second, zeros are extremely volatile investments—that is, their prices fluctuate dramatically with moves in economywide interest rates. As you'll see, not all zeros are uniformly volatile, and for active traders the volatility of zeros is an attractive advantage.

Third, the prices for zeros, even for years of identical maturity, vary widely, so you have to shop carefully.

Finally, commissions are an important consideration to buyers of zeros, and they are somewhat higher as a percentage of initial investment than are commissions for other investments. There are, however, ways to minimize commissions, and after a little study you'll conclude that zeros are fully worth their commissions.

The only thing that seems greater than investors' appetite for zeros is their appetite for information about them. To date, much of that information has been sketchy, offered only in sales literature from brokerages or from brief articles by financial writers in personal finance magazines or newspaper investment columns. There's been no single, comprehensive source of information about the total uses of zeros, and that's a situation this book wants to correct. *The New Dow Jones-Irwin Guide to Zero Coupon Investments* will acquaint you with the types of zero coupon securities and the strategies you can use to manage them.

The books is divided into two parts. Part 1 explains the different types of zero coupon investments, outlines their features pro and con, and deals with their facts and mechanics. We start by discussing the general nature of zeros—what they are, how they work, how to read their price quotations, and how to calculate their approximate yields. Part 2 discusses strategies for assimilating zeros into coherent portfolios. We'll place zeros in the context of the five portfolio elements and discuss their usefulness in specific types of accounts, such as the Uniform Gifts to Minors Account and the IRA. In addition, you'll see how zeros can help pattern portfolio planning around life events, such as midcareer crises, capitalizing a personal business, or arranging income for a time when your paycheck is less dependable. You'll learn the questions you need to ask when buying zeros and the terms you'll encounter when your questions are answered.

As we close out the decade of the 1980s, we find ourselves in a time of special economic uncertainty. This edition carries a Special Addendum on working with zeros during changing economies.

In the Glossary and Appendix you'll find definitions of common zero coupon terms, a discussion of the tax consequences of zeros, and a worksheet for managing your portfolio of zeros.

CONTENTS

PART 1

THE FEATURES OF ZERO COUPON INVESTMENTS

CHAPTER 1

THE BASICS OF ZERO COUPON INVESTMENTS

As we examine zero coupon investments in more detail you'll become conversant with their many singular features. For now, however, we're concerned with understanding the four basics of zeros—*price, yield, maturity,* and *par value.* These basics are frustratingly related in the case of zeros, but it's not difficult to sort out the influences after you understand them.

The price of a zero coupon security is influenced by the quality of the issuer. Quality refers to the likelihood of the issuer being able to pay off when the zero matures. Basically the quality of the zero equals the financial solvency of the issuer.

Price is also influenced by yield, just as yield is determined by price. Yield is your return for lending money. It's also the payment you receive to compensate for the risk of lending and for not consuming what you could have bought with the money you loaned. As a generality, the lower the price of a zero coupon investment, the higher is its yield (although, as we'll see, that's not always the case).

Yield is related to quality through the risk of default. That is, if you think someone has a very high likelihood of being able to repay your loan, you'll ask for less interest—a reduced yield—because risk of default is (in your opinion, anyway) reduced.

Yield on zeros is determined by price, and both price and yield are functions of time. As a general rule, the longer the maturity, the higher the yield because lenders assume greater risk in "lending long" and because they defer consumption for a longer period. Also, yield tends to increase with time because investors usually must be induced to hold their investments long term.

In the case of most zeros, however, prices and yields also are sensitive to the general level of interest rates in addition to the solvency of the issuer and the length of maturity. That's because zeros make only one payment of interest—at maturity—and must be held to maturity in order to receive that interest. To look at it another way, the yield at which you purchased a zero is locked in for the life of the security, whereas general interest rates in the economy rise and fall. If interest rates rise, investors could be investing elsewhere for market-level returns, and they'll possibly sell their zeros to take advantage of higher yields in other investments. As we'll see, however, zeros' high "opportunity cost" can be an advantage.

Maturity also affects prices and yields. Other considerations being equal, the longer the period before a zero matures, the lower its price will be and, as a consequence, the higher its yield will be— up to a certain time. Also, the longer the term of maturity, the greater the zero's opportunity cost and price fluctuations will be.

Nearly all zeros have a par value of $1,000, but there are some exceptions. Some zeros are indexed to other financial gauges such as the inflation rate or Treasury securities rates, so their par values may exceed $1,000 when they mature. These instruments will pay at least $1,000 upon maturity, however, except for EE Savings Bonds, which offer par values from $50 to $10,000 and are also indexed to the average interest rate on five-year Treasury securities. Their ultimate par values are difficult to determine, but we have devoted parts of several chapters to EE bonds. One type of zero, the U.S. Treasury bill, has a minimum par value of $10,000 and the minimum purchase is one bill. Zero coupon certificates of deposit have several par values, usually $1,000, $5,000, $10,000, and $100,000.

SURVEY OF RELATIONSHIPS

Let's take a look at the relationships we've established in isolation and then put them together.

First, quality is positively related to price. The higher the quality of the issuer, the higher the price of the zero will be compared to zeros of similar maturity from other issuers.

Second, quality is inversely related to yield. That follows, because price and yield are inversely related to each other. Higher prices mean lower yields. The higher the quality of the issuer, the lower the zero's yield will be compared to investments of lesser quality.

Price is inversely related to time: the longer the maturity, the lower the price will be.

Yield is usually related positively to time: the longer the maturity, the higher the yield will be.

Like the rose, par value is par value, a buck's a buck, and $1,000 is $1,000 except in those few instances when par value is more than $1,000 because it's determined by minimum purchase requirements—like T-bills with $10,000 minimums—or by sliding interest calculations, as in the case of zeros with yields geared to an index of some sort. These issues are special cases, and we'll discuss them fully later.

Before delving into the special cases, however, let's see how these considerations manifest themselves in public markets. First, let's take a look at a series of zero coupon bonds by the same issuer.

	Maturity Date	Price	Approx. Yield
CATS	1992	$723	8.25%
	1999	$403	9.50%
	2006–11	$183	10.5–7.25%

All of these issues are backed by U.S. government bonds, so quality of the issuer can't account for differences in prices and yields. You see most of the relationships confirmed. You see prices declining with time and yields increasing with time. There is, however, a perplexing aberration: the CATS of 2006–11. These zeros are unusual in several respects.

First, they feature two maturity dates—2006 and 2011. That's because these zeros are backed by Treasury bonds that are "callable" in 2006. In other words, during and after the year 2006, the government can (but not necessarily will) call these bonds back from owners prior to terminal maturity in 2011. Consequently, the CATS derived from these bonds are also callable. Call features are especially important with zero coupon municipal bonds, as we'll discuss in Chapter 4.

Second, although prices on these issues decline as maturity increases—the customary relationship—the yield increases only to 2006 and actually declines by 2011. This clearly isn't the customary relationship, for yields should increase with time. This aberration introduces two issues: yield to call and the effect of overall market relationships on zero coupon issues.

Whenever a zero is callable, investors must know the yield until the security is called because yields can vary dramatically when call provisions are imposed. Again, this is a more important issue with zero coupon municipals than with other zeros.

The effect of overall market relationships is a more complicated issue. It's difficult to say why the yield to maturity falls for the CATS of 2006–11, but the most likely explanation will be found in the economy.

Economies have a *term structure of interest rates* as a matter of course. In a highly inflationary economy, short-term rates—maturities under five years or so—may actually exceed long-term rates by several percentage points. That's because borrowers who issue securities would rather pay high rates for a short period than pay high rates for a long period. But even in stabler times, the structure of interest rates generally has a *yield elbow*. Interest rates in general will increase over some term—say, 20 years—and then decline modestly or sharply.

If you were to draw a line through a chart of interest rates, the line would resemble an arm rising over some period and then declining. The point of decline is the elbow, and whether it bends sharply or gradually, early in the term structure of interest rates or late, depends upon economic factors that are more megaeconomic than macroeconomic. It merely happens, and investors have to accept that it happens. Figure 1–1 illustrates the term structure of interest rates.

The horizontal axis represents time—in this hypothetical case, from six months to more than 20 years. The vertical axis represents yields available on U.S. Treasury securities. We've chosen Treasury securities because they're generally considered immune to default and, therefore, profitability considerations don't influence their prices

FIGURE 1-1
Sample Illustration: Term Structure of Interest Rates

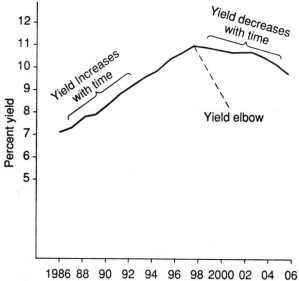

and yields as would be the case with corporate issues of identical maturity.

As you can see, yields increase out to a period of about 12 years, after which yields plateau and then dip a bit. The yield elbow occurs at about 12 years of maturity, indicating that the economy is offering its highest yields for 12-year maturities. Beyond maturities of 12 years, the economy does not offer commensurate yields to reward investing longer term in this example.

COMPARING DIFFERENT ZEROS

Thus far, our example has covered only one issue of zeros, and that issue was available in public markets, tradeable like any publicly listed security. Many types of zeros petition for your attention, so let's compare. In the table on the next page, we'll examine a range of zero coupon investments and hold the maturity at approximately 10 years.

Investment	Price	Approximate Interest
$10,000 Zero Coupon CD	$4,631	8.00%
$10,000 EE Savings Bond	$5,000	(see note)
$10,000 CATS of 1999	$3,950	8.74%
$10,000 Allied-Signal Zeros of 1999	$3,575	10.60%

Note: As you'll learn in the discussion of EE Savings Bonds, EEs pay a sliding rate of interest which increases the longer you hold the bond. EE bonds pay a minimum of 6 percent when held for their full 12-year maturity, and when held at least five years they pay 85 percent of the average interest rate for five-year Treasury notes.

In this case we've changed denominations to $10,000 just to vary examples a bit. Each of these investments has approximately the same maturity, varying only by a few months. For example, the Allied-Signal Corporation issue matures in late December 1999, whereas the CATS mature in mid-May 1999. Yet prices and yields differ markedly, as do other circumstances pertaining to each zero. These price and yield quotations are very approximate, changing daily, yet they illustrate some of the tradeoffs that investors make when buying zero coupon securities.

Note that the zero CD and the EE Savings Bonds have the highest prices and lowest yields. However, the former, being issued by an institution backed by the Federal Savings and Loan Insurance Corporation, and the latter, being an obligation of the U.S. government, are highly secure against default, and neither fluctuates in price as do the other zeros in our example. Further, the accreted interest on the zero CD is fully taxable, whereas the interest on the EE bond is exempt from state tax. These advantages are incorporated into the higher price and correspondingly lower yields of the zeros.

As you'd expect, the yield on the CATS is slightly lower than the yield on the corporate zero of the same maturity. That the CATS are derived from U.S. government securities probably explains the differential: better security against default. However, bear in mind that both issues will fluctuate in price, unlike the first two, and commissions aren't charged to purchase zero CDs and EE Savings Bonds.

Why would one type of investor prefer a lower-yielding zero over another? Much of the rest of this book is devoted to answering that question, but we can introduce some considerations that we'll cover at length later.

PREFERENCES AND STRATEGIES FOR ZEROS

We've already surmised that some investors are willing to pay a higher price and accept a lower yield because of the safety, stability, and absence of commissions associated with zero CDs and savings bonds. Such investors resent the commissions and resist the capital fluctuations of publicly traded zeros, nor would they go near some of the other types of zero coupon investments that we'll study.

Investors who buy zeros intending to hold them to maturity aren't concerned with interim capital fluctuations. All they care about is that their zeros mature to par value. Accordingly, you'd expect investors following the buy-and-hold strategy to prefer the highest yielding zero, which is the Allied-Signal Corporation zero in our example. For some investors, that would be the preferred investment because its yield is highest. However, other investors would prefer the CATS because of their claim against Treasury bonds. These buy-and-hold investors are willing to sacrifice a bit of yield for added security.

For another thing, the convenience of EE bonds and zero CDs (or other types of zeros) may offset their reduced yield for some investors. Some investors find the convenience of buying zeros where they bank or where they have their brokerage accounts to be worth a little yield. (By the way, the same can be said for buying other types of zeros: buying savings bonds where you work, convertible municipals from your municipal bond broker, or shares in a zero bond fund from a mutual fund family in which you already invest.)

Some investors aren't interested in the yield on zeros at all because they don't intend to hold them until maturity. They intend to play zeros for capital appreciation—an aggressive strategy that we'll look at—and to do so they must buy zeros traded in open markets or in markets maintained by brokers from whom they bought their zeros.

The zeros of Allied-Signal Corporation and the CATS are listed on public exchanges. Like all listed securities, including many other issues of zeros, markets are maintained by middlemen, and prices are established by the public's demand for the securities as well as by the conditions outlined at the start of this chapter. These zeros can be bought and sold any time because the public market maintains liquidity. Therefore, they're favored by aggressive investors because their mechanics make it possible to buy and sell them.

But some conditions might impair liquidity—ability to buy and sell—of other types of zeros. Those conditions dissuade aggressive investors, but it's also important for those who invest in zeros to understand them.

For example, EE Savings Bonds can't be redeemed before you've owned them for six months. That's the law, and there are no exceptions. But after six months you can sell them anywhere at a price established by the government, not by the market. Despite the many advantages of EE Savings Bonds, which you'll study in later chapters, they are absolutely illiquid for six months and their prices are determined by fiat, not by financial markets. Neither condition bothers some investors and investment strategies; both conditions are intolerable for others.

Next, some zeros don't have public or private markets. For example, a zero coupon certificate of deposit is a contractual obligation. You agree to leave funds on deposit for a specific period, at the end of which time the institution agrees to pay a specified face value. Under some conditions, if you redeem a zero CD before it matures, you will be subject to interest penalties. In effect, the zero CD generally isn't liquid, although some large denomination zero CDs and zero CDs purchased through brokerages are. Lack of liquidity doesn't bother investors following a buy-and-hold strategy, but it can trouble other investors greatly.

Another condition influencing liquidity pertains to zeros purchased from sponsoring brokerages. For each issue of a corporate or derivative zero that enters public markets, scores of other issues are purchased privately by financial institutions that sell them to customers. Most major brokerage firms maintain inventories of their own zeros or zeros from other institutions, including zero CDs plus corporate and derivative zeros. They frequently will maintain a market in these issues.

READING PRICE QUOTATIONS

It's time that you learned to read zero coupon bond quotations from the financial pages. If you buy zeros from some sources, you'll receive a conventional dollar price quotation and yield: the investment literature will read something like "$1,759 for a yield of 10.10 percent." But zeros are usually quoted in financial code. Here's a quotation for a corporate zero from *The Wall Street Journal,* although derivative zeros and municipal zeros are similarly quoted.

ISSUER	VOLUME	CLOSE	CHANGE
AlldC zr95	10	53-3/4	$-1/4$

The issuer is Allied-Signal Corporation. If you're perplexed about the identity of an issuer, check with a broker or consult a stock market quotation guide. The *zr* identifies the issue as a zero, and *95* is the maturity date of 1995. The 10 is trading volume—10 bonds or $10,000 in par value has changed hands—followed by the closing price and comparison with the previous day's close, off fractionally here.

To read price quotations, convert fractions to decimals. In this case, 53-3/4 becomes 53.75. Multiply by 10, giving 537.50. Add a dollar sign and you're done. The closing price of this zero on the New York Bond Exchange was $537.50. At that price, the bond was selling for $2.50 less than on the previous day.

Zero coupon municipal bonds are also quoted in dollars per hundred, which means you must multiply quotations by 10 to convert prices to $1,000 par value. In most instances, however, municipal zeros aren't quoted in fractions. For example:

Sam Rayburn TxMun Pwr Agy Pwr Sup Sys Rv 9/1/12 at 7.379

In this case, the issue is a revenue bond floated by the municipal power agency in Sam Rayburn, Texas, maturing in September 2012. You'll learn more about municipal zeros in Chapter 4. The item of interest is the price: 7.379. To decipher the figure, multiply by 10, giving 73.79. Add a dollar sign, and you've figured out that the zero can be bought for $73.79 per $1,000 par value.

A THUMBNAIL GUIDE TO CALCULATING YIELDS

For the most part, buying zeros presents no complicated mathematical problem. Purchase price is quoted by a dealer or in the financial pages. Your zeros will be worth $1,000 when they mature, because $1,000 is the customary par value of zeros. And usually you know the implied interest rate because your broker or sales literature has quoted it to you. Unfortunately, though, you may see a zero in the bond pages while your broker isn't available to figure the yield, or perhaps you'll want to confirm a quoted interest rate with your own calculations. Such occasions require you to calculate yield on a zero coupon security—the approximate yield, that is, because the accurate yield changes from minute to minute. Fortunately, most of us don't need to know the yield of a zero to the ultimate decimal, and all we need for a serviceable calculation is a compound interest table.

The basic idea behind the concept of accreted interest is that $1 to be received today is worth $1, whereas someone's promise to give you $1 tomorrow ought to be worth less than $1 to accommodate risk of lending, forsaken consumption, and a return for investing. A zero coupon security promises to pay $1,000 tomorrow for an investment today, so you'd expect it to sell for less than $1,000. How much less depends upon the circumstances we noted early on. The price for and yield of money received in the future is a *present value computation*, and you calculate the present value with the table labeled "Present Value of $1" from a compound interest table.

Some form of compound interest table is to be found in nearly every college finance book. For the novice, a useful text is *Compound Interest and Annuity Tables* by Jack C. Estes (New York: McGraw-Hill, 1976). Advanced students of interest and time value of money should read *The Dow Jones-Irwin Guide to Interest* by Lawrence R. Rosen (Homewood, IL: Dow Jones-Irwin, 1981). Also, modestly sophisticated pocket calculators have compound interest features that enable you to calculate yield without knowing what you're calculating.

In this case, what we're doing is estimating the interest rate, or yield. Price, maturity, and par value are known, but the interest yield created by the difference between price and par is unknown. Let's take the example of a hypothetical zero quoted at a price of $320 for maturity in approximately 11 years.

In establishing a price of $320, the market tells you that $1,000 to be received in 11 years from this issuer is worth $320 today. In other words, the present value of $1,000 is $320. Our question is, according to what rate of interest is $1,000 worth $320 today? You turn to a present value table in a book or compound interest tables, and through trial and error, under columns of figures for 11-year maturities, you find these entries:

Years	10% Nominal Annual Rate	10.5% Nominal Annual Rate	11% Nominal Annual Rate	11.5% Nominal Annual Rate
11	0.3418	0.3244	0.3079	0.2923

These numbers declare the present value of $1 to be received 11 years from now. To find the present value of $1,000, multiply by 1,000. Accordingly, at a 10.5 percent nominal rate of interest, $1,000 to be received 11 years from now is worth $324.40. At 11 percent nominal interest, $1,000 to be received 11 years from now is worth $307.90.

The price of $320 falls between the $324.40 that indicates a 10.5 percent yield and the $307.90 representing an 11 percent yield. Reasoning with given information about price and years to maturity, you see that today's price of $320 represents a yield between 10.5 and 11 percent and much closer to 10.5 percent than to 11 percent.

This figure is the approximate yield to maturity of the zero, the yield you'd receive if you held the zero for its full term of maturity. To find yield to call, substitute the call date for the maturity date.

We've used the present value schedule for semiannual compounding. Even though zeros are presumed to pay phantom annual interest, their yields and sometimes tax consequences are calculated using semiannual compounding tables, as they would be for coupon-paying bonds. Refer to the Appendix for a discussion of phantom taxes on zeros held outside tax-deferred plans.

SUMMARY

This chapter has provided the basics you need in order to understand the features and terminology of zero coupon investments. We've covered the essentials of price, yield, par value, and maturity and have introduced some concepts in comparing different types of zeros. In addition, you now have a basic understanding of how to read price quotations and how they translate into yields. The term structure of interest rates is a useful tool that helps you determine which maturities of zeros offer the highest yields. With this information behind you, it's time to examine the types of bonds it applies to.

CHAPTER 2

GOVERNMENT-BACKED AND DIRECTLY ISSUED TREASURY ZEROS

As you saw in the Introduction, CATS, TIGRs, and other financial felines are created from conventional Treasury bonds by stripping interest and principal portions of the bond certificate and selling each separately. The newly created instrument is derived from a previous bond and reoffered to buyers in its new form, so as a category they're called *derivative* or *reoffered zeros*.

These are not original issue zeros, which we'll cover in this and later chapters, because they are not originally issued as zero coupon securities, as are other types of corporate, government, municipal obligations. For the most part, their status as second generation bonds is a matter of more curiosity to finance students than to investors, but there is one term we have to raise: *government-backed*.

GOVERNMENT-BACKED ZEROS

Read any advertisement for the financial felines created by brokerage institutions, and you'll see they're billed as government-backed securities. The securities from which these zeros are derived are backed by the full faith and credit of the U.S. government. But the U.S. government and the Treasury Department do not back *the derivative zeros themselves* directly with their full faith and credit or taxing power.

When Merrill Lynch or Salomon Bros. or Shearson Lehman Hutton creates derivative zeros, it purchases the Treasury bonds from which the zeros are created. The Treasury bonds are backed by the full faith and credit of the U.S. government. The brokerage is the owner of the record, and the brokerage has the claim upon the Treasury backing, not the investor who bought the derivative zeros. The brokerage places the Treasury bonds in permanent escrow with a major bank. These escrowed funds are then stripped of principal and interest and reoffered as zeros. The escrowed bonds are the backing for the zeros, not the Treasury outright. The Treasury backs the escrowed bonds from which the zeros are created, but the Treasury doesn't back the zeros themselves.

However, the advertisers are not being outright misleading. In this context, *government-backed* is merely financial shorthand. The only way these bonds will default is if the U.S. Treasury repudiates its debt, if the escrow agent does something dishonest with the escrowed securities, and if the brokerage refuses to make payment when the zeros are due. None of this is likely to happen singly, and fundamentally all three parties would have to renege simultaneously before the LIONS or TIGRs or CATS would be out of the bag that you're left holding. So you can use the term *government-backed* honestly but somewhat imprecisely, and you can think of financial felines as close proxies for Treasury bonds with all of the security due a Treasury obligation.

Characteristics

Like all of the zeros you'll examine, derivative zeros have four important characteristics: price, interest rate, maturity, and par value. As you saw in Chapter 1, these four characteristics are interrelated.

Price is straightforward enough. You pay what you pay whether you're buying the zeros in public markets or through a broker's inventory, and you learned how to translate price quotations in Chapter 1. But as long as we're on the subject of prices, we need to repeat an important point: always shop around. It's not at all uncommon to find derivatives of similar or identical maturity selling at considerable discrepancy in prices.

Derivative zeros come in virtually as many maturities as do government bonds—which shouldn't be surprising, considering where derivatives originate.

Par value is an easy subject when you're talking about government-backed zeros. It's $1,000 for all of them. No one has yet created derivatives with sliding interest payments resulting in par of more than $1,000.

Advantages

The chief advantage to derivative zeros is their high security against default. Many investors like to hold derivatives in Individual Retirement Accounts (IRA), and some investors like to purchase long-term zeros to maximize capital accumulations. You can buy long-term derivatives with confidence, knowing there's an exceedingly slim likelihood of default.

The close proximity of derivative zeros to Treasury bonds makes them attractive to aggressive investors who want short-term price appreciation from fluctuations in interest rates. Highly secure against default, zeros don't have default risk built into their prices, which are determined almost exclusively by the term structure of interest rates. As you'll see when we discuss the uses for zeros in each of the five portfolio components, aggressive investors prefer derivatives for quick gains because they are cleaner interest rate plays.

Derivatives' broad selection of maturities serves investors of many orientations, not merely those who want long-term zeros in a buy-and-hold IRA strategy or those who expect to trade them frequently for price appreciation. Short-term and intermediate-term maturities, those of less then 5 years and from 5 to 10 years, are useful in many portfolio strategies. We'll cover them in separate chapters devoted to zero coupon investments and each of the portfolio elements.

Disadvantages

The disadvantages of derivatives are the same as for almost any zero coupon security. First, they are intensely volatile. Felines are exceedingly sensitive to interest rates—more so than other bonds. Derivatives with near-term maturities are less sensitive to price fluctuations, but even they act more erratically than conventional bonds of similar maturity. Therefore, if you're going to invest in derivatives, you have to tolerate capital fluctuations.

Second, as we've already mentioned, prices for derivatives of similar or identical maturity can vary widely among sponsors and markets. Even though all derivatives are virtually the same product, price differences can be 25 percent or more. This fact makes shopping for the best prices a more difficult and time-consuming proposition.

Third, commissions can be a formidable charge when you're buying derivatives, and commissions (or their equivalent) aren't uniform. Commissions are important to buyers of zeros because they're fairly high as a percentage of investment, zeros don't pay interim interest to offset commissions, and commissions can reduce yield to maturity.

Probably the least expensive way to buy zeros is directly from the inventory of the sponsoring brokerage. When you buy CATS on the open market from a full-service broker, you'll pay a straight commission. (At present, other felines aren't sold through listed exchanges, although Merrill Lynch has shown some intention of listing its TIGRs.) If you buy them from the sponsor, you'll be charged a basis price. Basis pricing is the equivalent of a commission, but it's usually less. Also, you can buy zeros from some discount brokerages—those that offer only order execution—for a flat fee plus a small charge per bond.

The most frequently cited "disadvantage" of zeros is their failure to pay current income while they generate a current tax liability from phantom interest. Of course, many recommended investments, such as real estate, precious metals, collectibles, and many growth stocks, pay no current income, yet they often involve taxes, carrying charges, insurance fees, safe deposit rentals, appraisal costs, and other detractions.

In addition, many investors don't regard phantom interest taxation as particularly burdensome. We'll mention this point in other contexts, but it's important that we mention it here because many investors think derivatives are appropriate only for tax-deferred accounts. They're wrong.

First, be honest about what really happens with investment income. Too often, you spend it instead of reinvesting it, and you wind up with little more than your initial capital. You also pay taxes on that dissipated income. Even if you have to pay taxes on phantom interest yearly, at least you'll have capital accumulations when your zeros mature. That's better than looking back on all the coupon interest payments you've squandered while you're totaling up your yearly interest payments.

Second, investors are accustomed to paying taxes on interest income that's reinvested, and in effect your phantom interest payments are reinvested for compounded growth as zeros approach maturity. Thus, the tax situation on zeros is no more onerous than is customary for reinvested income.

Third, proposed revisions to the tax code promise to remove tax deferral features of other types of investments. Many economists and politicians have proposed taxing the hitherto untaxed accumulations in annuities and the capital growth in other types of insurance products. If enacted, these proposals are but a step away from taxation on the unreceived appreciation in stocks, homes, rental property, real estate, and other investments that appreciate in value while you own them. If these investments become taxable as current income, zeros will be no more disadvantaged than these vehicles, and they'll always have predictable accumulations in their favor, which no other investment offers.

ORIGINAL ISSUE TREASURY ZEROS— EE SAVINGS BONDS

At bottom, today's zero coupon bonds, including some of the more sophisticated alternatives we'll examine in later chapters, are little more than extensions of the original zero coupon bond, the Series E (now Series EE) Savings Bond. What's more, the original zero coupon bond is still the easiest, most accessible, and most convenient of all the zeros available today.

Even though the EE bond is the grandfather of all zeros, it has several singular features that makes it different from later generations. Or, to be more accurate, EE Savings Bonds contain nearly all the features that contemporary zeros have inherited singly. Thus, EE bonds are the least like any single issue of zeros, but they're the most like all of them examined together.

Consequently, we have to start with EE bonds. By understanding them and their uses, you can understand the zeros that followed them, and in understanding the usefulness of other zeros, you will understand EE bonds.

The familiar EE bond works like the zeros that we discussed in the Introduction. It's sold at discount from par value and pays accreted interest as the difference between purchase price and par value of the bond. However, there are several major differences between EE bonds and other zeros.

- First, par values of EE bonds are $50, $75, $100, $200, $500, $1,000, $5,000, and $10,000, whereas par for other zeros is nearly always $1,000.
- Second, you buy all EEs at half of their par value. A $50 EE bond costs $25. A $10,000 EE bond costs $5,000. With other zeros, you pay a price that decreases with the lengthening maturity of the bond.
- Third, the maturity of all EE bonds is 12 years. Other zeros, of course, have longer and shorter maturities, with correspondingly lower and higher prices.
- Fourth, EE bonds purchased after November 1982 pay a rate of interest that increases the longer you hold the bond. Most other zeros pay a fixed rate of interest determined by price at the time of purchase regardless of their maturity, although some original issue corporate zeros also pay indexed interest.

There's another aspect to sliding EE bond interest: held five years, EE bonds pay 85 percent of the average yield on five-year U.S. Treasury notes and are guaranteed to earn no less than 6 percent. Whenever average yields on five-year Treasuries exceed 6 percent, a $50 EE bond matures to more than $50, as will the other denominations. Therefore, with EE bonds par value is an approximation, not a fixed figure.

EE Savings bonds differ from their descendants in other ways. For one thing, EE bonds will never be worth less than purchase price even if cashed before maturity, nor will they ever be worth more than their scheduled value as determined by how long you've owned them. Because EE bond prices don't vary inversely with interest rates, they don't offer dramatic short-term gains, but they never suffer capital losses. Therefore, they're ideal for investors who demand capital stability.

Second, you may declare accreted interest from EE bonds as it accrues yearly, *or* you may postpone declaring interest until the bond matures or is cashed. Thus, EE bonds are an exception to tax laws that require you to pay tax on phantom interest. Also, accreted interest from EE Savings Bonds is exempt from state, city, regional, and local taxes because EE bonds are U.S. government obligations.

Third, EE bonds paying accreted interest may be exchanged for HH bonds paying coupon interest. The convertibility of EE bonds is such an attractive advantage for some investors that we have part of a chapter devoted to it and to a similar investment, the zero coupon convertible municipal bond.

But perhaps one of the greatest advantages of EE bonds is that their disadvantages really aren't disadvantages. Savings bonds do have impaired liquidity because you must hold them six months before you can cash them. For long-term investors, temporarily impaired liquidity is no consideration because they aren't turning investments around every six months. In any event, after six months the bonds are liquid at any tellers' cage, and the offsetting advantage to impaired liquidity is stability of principal. Another point often made against EE Savings Bonds is that they pay less interest than other types of zeros. However, EE bonds are indexed to five-year Treasury notes, so their yields become more competitive the longer you own them.

ORIGINAL ISSUE TREASURY ZEROS—T-BILLS

Treasury bills—more frequently called T-bills—are short-term direct obligations of the U.S. government that mature in 13, 26, or 52 weeks. The term *bills* denotes the brevity of their maturity, as government notes usually mature in less than 10 years and government bonds usually mature more than 10 years after they're issued.

Long-time favorites of money managers and conservative investors, T-bills are one of the safest investments and are often used in place of cash by many financial institutions. As direct obligations of Uncle Sam, they are the nearest thing to default-proof, and their short-term maturities assure that there is little danger of capital loss. Their one drawback is their high cost—$10,000.

T-bills have many purposes, the foremost being that their liquidity, stability, and yields are perfect for the savings component of your portfolio. However, they are excellent parking lots for capital awaiting investment, and their capital stability plus government backing makes them excellent investment havens during economic uncertainty.

STRIPS

In August 1984, the Treasury Department recognized the incredible popularity of derivative zeros (at that time more than $45 billion worth of Treasury bonds had been stripped to create derivative zeros) and undertook administrative actions that made it easier for financial institutions to create them. In February 1985, the Treasury's action resulted in the creation of STRIPS (Separate Trading of Registered Interest and Principal of Securities).

STRIPS are great for financial institutions, but they're a bane to financial writers because they're difficult to describe. In a nutshell, STRIPS aren't bonds; they're blip on computer tape—a special designation on certain regular issues of Treasury bonds that enables them to be sold as regular Treasury bonds and also facilitates financial institutions' severing the coupon and interest payments to sell each separately.

The designation is called a CUSIP number, named for the American Banking Association Committee on Uniform Securities Identification Procedures. Every security—stocks, government bonds, corporate bonds—has a distinct CUSIP number by which it is identified. Under the STRIPS program, certain government bonds selected by the Treasury have multiple CUSIP numbers. With these specially identified bonds, the whole bond—principal and interest—has one CUSIP number, and each component of the bond—the principal and each coupon—also has its own CUSIP number. Having multiple CUSIP numbers makes it easier for financial institutions to resell severed interest and principal payments because each already has a preestablished CUSIP number.

The problem is further complicated because STRIPS are direct issues of the U.S. government, but they aren't issued by the U.S. government, and private investors can't buy them directly. They're for sale only to financial institution that have book-entry securities accounts with the Federal Reserve. In other words, STRIPS exist on computer tape only, and they may be purchased only by financial institutions that are on file with the Fed's computer.

However, financial institutions can resell their purchases of STRIPS to individual investors under their trade names. For instance, Shearson Lehman Brothers, the international brokerage institution, sells STRIPS under its trade name TINTS, standing for Treasury Interest.

For our purposes, we can regard STRIPS exactly as we regard any other derivative zero, because that's the way you'll end up with them. They work exactly like the derivative zeros we discussed in Chapter 2, and the same circumstances apply regarding maturity, safety, commissions, and other features.

STRIPS produce phantom taxable interest yearly, so if you hold them outside IRAs and Keogh Plans you'll be expected to declare a portion of accreted interest each year. However, phantom interest on STRIPS is exempt from state and local tax, which isn't the case with derivative Treasury zeros. Fortunately, IRS Publication 1212 will reveal the phantom taxable interest due on STRIPS held outside IRAs and Keoghs, discussed more fully in the Appendix.

SUMMARY

Treasury zeros, both derivative and direct issues, offer investors ultimate assurance against default along with the many advantages that all zeros carry as a category of investment. CATS and TIGRs, T-bills, and STRIPS are widely traded in public markets, making them easily accessible. The EE Savings Bond, the grandfather of zero coupon securities, is one of the most maligned zeros, but it, too, offers exceptional advantages, including some we've not yet discussed.

CHAPTER 3

CORPORATE ZEROS

When zeros became widely traded in public markets during the early 1980s, several corporations promptly took advantage of investors' enthusiasm for the concept. Original issue corporate zeros are exactly like derivative zeros in their particulars except, of course, that they're backed only by the issuer's promise to pay par value upon maturity and aren't underpinned by another type of bond.

Accordingly, corporate zeros present some additional issues in analyzing them. Further, the notion of "corporate paper" is not confined to the customary types of zeros nor to customary types of corporations. The concept of securities issued at an original issue discount has long pertained to certain types of corporate debt, and as new types of zeros have emerged, so have new types of corporations emerged to offer them.

COMMERCIAL PAPER

Well-capitalized investors and financial institutions have been dealing in several types of corporate zeros for many years. Commercial paper short-term obligations of corporations), repurchase agreements (sell-and-buy-back arrangements with government bonds), and even commercial letters of credit (issued by one financial institution and saleable at a discount to another) legitimately qualify as zero coupon securities. They are retailed at a price lower than their terminal value—*par* isn't exactly the right word—and they come due—*mature* isn't exactly descriptive either—at a higher price.

The chief advantages of commercial paper are capital stability and market-level rates of return. Being exceedingly short in maturity, nearly always less than a year and often within a few hours or days, their capital fluctuations are minimal. Further, markets for these types of commercial zeros are broad and competitive, so their accreted interest represents state-of-the-moment yields for short-term yields.

For private investors, however, the initial purchase price of these instruments is beyond reach, for they're customarily denominated in the millions of dollars. As an indirect investor in money market funds and other types of zero coupon funds, you can participate in portfolios of these zeros, as we'll discuss in later chapters.

ZERO COUPON CERTIFICATES OF DEPOSIT

Like conventional interest-paying CDs, zero CDs are direct issues of the sponsoring bank, S&L, or credit union. They are sold at discounts from par to mature in a fixed number of years. Generally, the disadvantage of zero CDs is their limited range of maturities. With few exceptions, zero CDs are offered in five-year maturities at a price of $500 per $1,000 par value and 12-year maturities for a price of $250.

However, some depositaries with a national customer base have expanded their range of maturities and par values. It is possible to buy zero CDs from a few depositaries in maturities of 1, 5, 10, 12, and 20 years at yields that increase with the term of deposit. Par values of these broader access zero CDs range from $1,000 to $100,000 and information about them occasionally appears in *The Wall Street Journal* and other financial publications.

Zero CDs carry the advantages of known purchase price, known yield, and known accumulations that are featured by other zeros. They are also immune to price fluctuations, which makes them desirable for conservative investors, and they require no commissions for purchase.

These advantages aside, zero coupon CDs are not generally useful by themselves. Excluding the jumbo denominations of $100,000, zero CDs are usually illiquid before maturity. Their illiquidity makes them useful only as a kind of hands-off extension of your savings component. However, zero CDs can be excellent adjuncts to other zero coupon investments.

Say, for example, that you can't find an attractive corporate or derivative zero with a 12-year maturity. You could select a zero CD from a bank or brokerage and blend it in with your other holdings of zeros. As you'll see later, blending different types of zeros provides optimum usefulness and balance in your portfolio.

You can hold zero CDs as you would any other CD, and interest will be taxable yearly or upon maturity, depending upon when the CD was issued. Zero CDs issued after 1984 are taxable yearly according to formulas discussed in the Appendix. Zero CDs held in IRAs and Keoghs compound tax-deferred until you make withdrawals from your account.

In addition to zero CDs purchased directly from a sponsoring depositary, you can purchase reoffered CDs from banks and brokerages that purchase "jumbo CDs" from the original issuers and break them into smaller denominations for resale. The brokerage's procedure is essentially the same as for reoffering T-bonds as CATS and TIGRs.

You purchase these derivative CDs from the offering brokerage for prices, yields, and par values determined by the offering. Generally, original issue CDs and reoffered CDs carry FDIC or FSLIC insurance, so they're highly secure against default. Such assurances aside, however, you might be highly skeptical about any investment involving today's troubled banking industry. If so, consider Treasury-backed zeros and investment grade corporate or municipal zeros as alternatives.

Sometimes the offering brokerage will make a market in its reoffered CDs, which means you have some liquidity without interest penalties. However, if you sell a zero CD back to the sponsor, you'll be at its mercy in the price you receive. Your sales price could be lower than your purchase price, especially for longer maturities.

ZERO COUPON CORPORATE BONDS

Following the advent of derivative zeros, corporations were quick to seize upon their advantages and popularity by issuing their own original issue zeros. In the case of corporations, there was a special attraction for hopping on the zero bandwagon: whereas private investors must usually declare phantom taxable interest yearly even though they don't receive it until maturity, corporations may claim a tax deduction for phantom interest as if they'd actually paid it.

Although the dollar volume of corporate zeros is small when

compared to the multibillions of derivative and municipal zeros, a growing number of corporations have issued zero coupon debt. If you go through the New York Bond Exchange Listings in *The Wall Street Journal* or in your daily newspaper, you'll see that corporations like Allied-Signal, Bank of America, Cities Service, General Mills, GMAC, and Merrill Lynch (its own corporate debt, not its TIGRs) have zeros listed on public exchanges. As you would expect, this corporate debt features a range of maturities and prices. The American Exchange bond market also trades a few corporate zeros.

Again, these zeros operate like all the other zeros you've studied, except that they are backed only by the profitability of the issuing corporation. Just like derivative zeros, their principal characteristics are price, yield, par value, and maturity. Quotations for corporate zeros are translated in the manner you learned in Chapter 1, and their yields are also calculated in the manner described there.

Corporate zeros do have a few singular characteristics, however. Some corporate zeros feature sliding interest rates geared to the profitability of the issuer or to an index such as the consumer price index or the rates on Treasury bonds. Although nearly all corporate zeros feature $1,000 par, indexed corporate zeros may mature to more than $1,000. Further, a special type of corporate zeros is convertible into the common or preferred stock of the issuer. Convertibility gives investors the chance to profit from price appreciation of the underlying shares as well as price appreciation from decreases in interest rates. We'll look further at convertible corporate zeros in a special chapter devoted to convertibles.

Because they aren't underpinned by government securities, corporate zeros are vulnerable to default. Further, their prices are influenced by the issuer's profitability and by the general course of interest rates. This combination makes them less secure and more volatile than derivative zeros.

ANALYZING CORPORATE ZEROS

Because of these twin drawbacks, corporate zeros present a more complicated problem in investment analysis. Any basic investment text can give you a thumbnail course in debt analysis, but here are a few particulars you can use in analyzing corporate zeros.

First, check the subordination of zeros to other debt of the issuer.

Corporate bonds—actually, most are debentures—have junior and senior issues. As the terms imply, senior debt receives preference for payment if the corporation goes under. Junior debt is paid after senior debt, and most corporations have several layers of junior debt. Most, but not all, corporate zeros are junior debt. That doesn't mean you should avoid them; it merely means you need to look at the next step in the analysis.

That next step is to check the coverage ratios. This information is available from Standard & Poor's and Moody's guides to corporate debt, from Value Line stock guides, and from your broker. A coverage ratio measures the relationship of corporate assets to corporate debt—not only physical assets like plant and equipment, but also cash and near-cash assets like T-bills held in the corporate coffers. Coverage ratios give you an idea of how easily a corporation could cover its debt if necessary. Generally, a 1:1 ratio is acceptable, although many investors want a 2:1 ratio. A 2:1 ratio means that two dollars of corporate assets or cash cover each dollar of debt.

As a form of financial shorthand, you can ask what the corporation's debt rating is. As we've mentioned, independent rating agencies like Moody's and Standard & Poor's rate corporate debt for assurance against default. Given so many attractive derivative zeros available, there's no reason to accept less than A-rated corporate zeros. The slight advantage in yield over derivative zeros probably won't compensate for increased risk of default.

As you'll see in later chapters, corporate zeros can be used in the same strategies as derivative and other original issue zeros. They can be purchased for a buy-and-hold strategy, bought for aggressive gains, included in IRAs and Keoghs, and added to Uniform Gifts to Minors Accounts. As a generality, however, derivative zeros offer a wider range of maturities, and they are not influenced by profitability considerations. These two facts compel many investors to prefer derivatives over corporates.

FEDERAL NATIONAL MORTGAGE ASSOCIATION ZEROS

The Federal National Mortgage Association—better known as Fannie Mae—has issued several categories of indebtedness under its charter as a tax-paying, shareholder-owned corporation whose assets (more

than $90 billion in home mortgages) make it the third largest corpo-
ration in the United States. Although Fannie Mae is always adamant
in declaring that its debt is not a direct obligation of the U.S. government, most investors regard its obligations on a plane with government securities, and Fannie Mae debt is rated AAA.

Fannie Mae's best-known investment is a pass-through bond that
represents interest and principal payments on millions of mortgages.
However, with the advent of zero coupon investments, Fannie Mae
has begun to issue some of those, too.

In late 1984, Salomon Bros. and Nomura Securities International
underwrote a $6.7 billion offering of Federal National Mortgage
Association zero coupon subordinated capital debentures maturing in
2019. Since then, Fannie Mae has issued several series of what it calls
Capital Debentures, its trade name for its zero coupon debt. These are
original issue zeros from a private corporation that is presumed to be
able to call upon the backing of the U.S. government. Consequently,
they're regarded as a close proxy for CATS, TIGRs, and other
derivative zeros even though they are not, strictly speaking, backed
by the government. Like all zeros they're sold at deep discounts from
par, and the minimum face value you can buy is $5,000.

Capital Debentures can be purchased without commission from
the underwriters. Fannie Mae has said that it intends to apply for listing on the New York Bond Exchange. Assuming listing is approved,
Fannie Mae's Capital Debentures will be bought and sold like any
publicly traded zero, and as a zero coupon investor you can investigate them for your portfolio.

COLLATERALIZED MORTGAGE OBLIGATIONS

A security similar to the Fannie Mae Capital Debentures, Collateralized Mortgage Obligations (CMOs) are a recent financial innovation that takes pools of private mortgages and restructures them.
However, CMOs can have a variety of issuers, which means you'll
have to investigate their investment merits according to techniques
we've discussed for corporate original issue zeros.

CMOs are akin to derivative zeros in that they are created
from another type of security called a mortgage-backed pass-through
(MBS). Most such securities pay conventional coupon interest at regular intervals, usually monthly rather than semiannually. However,

the final class of CMOs—that is, the last security in the series issued, often called a tranche—is a Z-piece. It is sold like a conventional zero at a deep original issue discount.

The Z-piece (the Z presumably stands for zero) pays accreted interest only upon maturity. Consequently, it can be issued and purchased just like any of the zeros we've discussed. Remember, however, that there is as yet no public market for this type of zero even though they're coming to market from underwriters more frequently in the late 1980s. At present, markets are still maintained by the issuer, often a bank, mortgage institution, or S&L in addition to an investment banker. They may not be as liquid as other types of zeros until such time as they are listed.

"GOVERNMENT CORPORATIONS"

What some observers have called "privatization of government services" is a continuing process that's created many zero-issuing corporations that are related to federal government services and programs. These "government corporations," as they are derisively called, resemble Fannie Mae in that they are owned by shareholders who buy their corporate stock on listed exchanges. Other types of government corporations aren't corporations, but they are governmental agencies that issue debt, including zeros, more or less autonomously and for support of private sector enterprises.

Among the "corporate" zeros available to you are those of the Student Loan Marketing Association (Sallie Mae), the Federal Intermediate Credit Bank, and the Federal Farm Credit System. Some of their zeros are short-term and range from 5-day to 30-day discounted notes similar to T-bills. Other types are more conventional, carrying maturities of many years.

SUMMARY

There is scarcely a debtor in the economy who hasn't issued some form of zero coupon security. Corporate zeros allow you to participate in a greater number of markets while taking advantage of the benefits that zeros provide.

What's even better from the viewpoint of the private investor, issuers have become more innovative in the types of zeros they're offering to the public. The next chapter is devoted to another popular original issue zero, the zero coupon municipal bond. After you look at municipal zeros, you'll examine two other types of zero coupon investments, namely, convertible zeros and zero coupon funds.

CHAPTER 4

ZERO COUPON
MUNICIPAL BONDS

For some investors, federally taxable phantom yearly interest is a great drawback to owning zeros outside tax-deferred retirement accounts. But that's no reason to avoid zeros altogether. Zero coupon municipal bonds provide the same advantages of other zeros as well as exemption from federal taxation. Municipal zeros might even be more attractive than zeros in your tax-deferred retirement accounts.

Municipal zeros work exactly like their fully taxable brethren. However, the difference between their purchase price and par value is federally untaxed accreted interest. Unlike the situation with corporate and derivative zeros, Uncle Sam doesn't expect you to pay tax on phantom interest declared yearly on your Federal 1040, although under the post-1986 tax laws you must declare the phantom yearly interest from municipal bonds as an informational item. Your state may tax accreted interest; tax subjects are covered in the Appendix.

Conventionally, municipal securities are considered suitable only for investors in 30-percent-plus tax brackets. Many people argue that reducing the highest tax brackets would destroy the attractiveness of municipals for many investors. You need not be so conventional, however, in your thinking. Regardless of their tax brackets, many investors can benefit from municipal zeros.

ADVANTAGES OF MUNICIPAL ZEROS

Zero coupon municipal bonds have emerged as one of the most intelligent and popular of the investments to follow the Tax Reform Act of 1986. One reason is that Congress destroyed the attractiveness of many competing investments. Following tax reform, stock gains became fully taxable as earned income, and limited partnerships were virtually banished as tax write-offs. Other measures in that legislation also affected investment choices and income. IRA contributions were no longer universally deductible, and returns in Uniform Gifts to Minors Accounts became taxable in some cases at parents' rates. To make the sad story short, zero coupon municipal bonds were left as one of the few remaining investments with some tax favor.

In addition, Congress effectively assured that Americans would pay more in federal income tax by broadening the definition of fully taxable income. With many types of investment income taxable as earned income and with many former credits, deductions, and tax offsets eliminated, middle-class Americans found their out-of-pocket tax payments to Uncle Sam increasing by 30 percent. Investors and wage earners suddenly discovered that the federally untaxed returns of municipal zeros produced much more appealing returns.

Moreover, the October 1987 stock market debacle has convinced many people that the "should" and "ought to" predictions for stock market growth are a very undependable dialect. Rudely awakened to the fact that stocks don't provide dependable returns, investors found the predictable accumulations of municipal zeros (in fact, of all zeros) to be very appealing.

Finally, many advisors earnestly recommend that every working American contribute to an IRA. As a result of the new tax laws, many Americans can no longer deduct those contributions, and so this recommendation has become arguable. Therefore, many former IRA investors now buy zero coupon municipals instead of making a yearly IRA contribution. They've shifted the focus of their retirement planning in favor of municipal zeros, which still provide tax-favored accumulations.

EVALUATING QUALITY OF MUNICIPAL ZEROS

Safety against default is greater when the zeros are *general obligations* of an issuing state. A general obligation zero is backed by the taxing power of the state issuing it. Occasionally, zeros are backed by lesser tax authorities—a city or a regional tax agency—or zeros' interest will be paid from certain types of taxes or fees, such as school levies or highway tolls.

Project bonds are backed by revenues expected from the municipal project, such as a university dormitory, housing construction, a sewer system, a public power project, or a highway authority. Project zeros are better known by their financially correct names specified in their issuing prospectus, but they are similar in that accreted interest is paid from revenues financed by the borrowed capital. Because these projects have to make money before you're paid, they are generally less secure than zeros with interest paid by the taxing authority of the state.

As is the case with corporate zeros, assurance against default is estimated by independent rating agencies like Moody's or Standard & Poor's, which assign grades specifying the safety of the issue. These agencies study the debt coverage and financial standing of the issuing state or authority and encapsulate their findings in financial shorthand that reflects their analysis.

The highest rating is AAA, which indicates maximum assurance against default in the opinion of the rater. Subordinate ratings, like AA or A, indicate high quality issues with slightly less assurance against default, and BBB is the lowest rating for "investment grade" securities. There are so many good quality municipal zeros that there's no reason to accept less than an A rating. For long-term zeros, most investors will accept nothing lower than AA.

There are other circumstances that will merit a AAA rating. For example, some zeros are "escrowed," which means that the issuer has purchased U.S. government bonds or has deposited compensating funds in a bank to serve as collateral against the zero coupon debt.

Another assurance against default is afforded by "insured" municipals, which carry a AAA rating because of their "insurance." Municipal bond insurance is not insurance as you normally think of life or casualty insurance—that is, it isn't a payment for loss. It is a financial guarantee of additional backing for payment of principal and interest.

If, for some reason, a revenue or taxing authority is unable to pay accreted interest or repay principal, insured municipals can call upon the promise of agencies like the Municipal Bond Insurance Association and others to make good upon payment. Because of their advanced assurance against default, AAA-insured municipals usually carry lower interest than lesser-rated zeros. However, most investors gladly sacrifice a point or less in yield for greater assurance against default, particularly when investing long term.

CALL PROVISIONS AND CALL PROTECTION

Municipal issues are often "callable" at a certain point in their lives, meaning that the issuer can redeem this debt before it matures. Callable zeros can be an advantage or a disadvantage, depending upon the *price to call* and *yield to call*.

If a municipal zero is callable, its prospectus or literature from a broker will specify a date of callability, a price at which the issue can be redeemed, and sometimes a yield to that date. The price will be either a percentage of compound accreted value to date or a dollar amount.

For example, let's say that a zero costs $200 in 1989, is callable in 1999 at 102 percent of compound accreted value, and matures at $1,000 in 2009. In specifying call provisions in this manner, the issuer has assumed that the zero will produce a steady price increase each year of its life. This, of course, is the issuer's mathematical assumption, not necessarily your actual investment experience.

In this example, the issuer computes that the zero will increase in price by $40 per year as it marches to maturity ($1,000 minus $200 divided by 20 years equals $40 per year). In 1999, 10 years after issue, the compound accreted value to date is estimated to be $600 ($200 purchase price + $40 times 10 years). In 1999, the zero can be called for 102 percent of that figure, or $612.

Alternately, zeros with otherwise identical features to the example above might be callable at a specific price greater than, less than, or equal to compound accreted value to that date. In such cases, that call price is specified in the bond covenant or investment literature.

In both examples, if the zero is called in 1999, you receive the call price for each bond you own. That price will produce a yield to call which also may be less than, greater than, or equal to yield to maturity. Usually, yield to call is specified in the bond covenant or investment literature. If it isn't, you can calculate it by using the present value tables we've already discussed, substituting years to call for years to maturity. Otherwise, ask your broker—pointedly—what yield to call is.

You must always be concerned with yield to call. In general, you want a yield to call that is competitive with yields to maturity of other bonds that mature when the zero is callable. That is, you'd like a zero callable in, say, six years to yield a rate competitive with a bond maturing in six years. Naturally, you also want a yield to call that is competitive with other yields to call on other securities with similar call dates. Practically speaking, when you find that neither is the case, there's not much you can do about it except refuse to purchase the zero. Call features are fixed and will not change because of your preferences.

You always must assume your zero will be called, but the fact that an issue is callable doesn't mean that your particular zeros will be called. Sometimes an entire issue is callable, and sometimes an issue will feature *serial call,* which means that some bonds in the total issue can or will be redeemed at earlier or later times than other bonds in the issue. Sometimes an issuer fully intends to call its zeros, and at other times the issuer merely wants the option of calling them if there is an advantage to doing so.

As a general rule, call serves the issuer of a zero, not the buyer. Call provisions are a means by which the issuer can redeem debt and lower its interest payments if the economy permits lower rates. On the other hand, the investor benefits most by holding a zero compounding at a higher rate when economywide interest rates fall. In other words, the very time the bond is most attractive to the investor is the time it is least attractive to the issuer and therefore also the time the issuer is most likely to call the bond.

Call protection is the period of time remaining between the date you purchased the bond and the date it is callable. When initially offered, most general obligation municipal zeros are not callable for 10 years. If you buy them new, you have a decade before the bond is eligible to be called. That decade is your period of call protection. Project bonds, particularly zeros that finance housing or construction projects, may have *extraordinary call* through which your call protection is shortened.

When you buy existing zeros that have been on the market awhile, however, those bonds will be closer to call, just as they are closer to maturity. Consequently, your period of call protection is reduced. For a more detailed discussion of call protection on zeros and other municipal bonds, read *The Personal Investor's Complete Book of Bonds,* also written by your author.

MUNICIPAL ZEROS FOR LESSER-TAXED INVESTORS

Conventional wisdom argues that investors in the lower tax brackets should buy fully taxable zeros because their lower personal tax liability makes fully taxable zeros more attractive on an after-tax basis. Or more simply, lesser taxed investors don't enjoy the full benefits of interest exemption from federal tax. Let's look at this conventional wisdom critically.

First, your income, and therefore your tax burden, generally increases as you mature in your career. Accordingly, the municipal zeros you buy today will produce greater after-tax returns as your tax bracket increases.

Second, tax brackets and tax laws aren't cast in stone. During the past quarter century, Congress has changed the tax laws 19 times, and with each change, tax rates have increased and, most recently, the definition of taxable income has been broadened. Every informed expectation for 1989 and beyond is that Congress will increase rates and further broaden the base of fully taxable income. All of this means you pay and will pay higher federal taxes, and in turn that means federally untaxed interest from municipal zeros again will become more advantaged for the future.

Third, you must consider municipal zeros if you will invest at all. No other investment offers their advantages of predictable accumulations, tax favor, and liquidity. The goals for which people generally invest are the goals served by municipal zeros.

Fourth, you must consider municipal zeros for selected investment situations, particularly as an adjust or replacement for tax-deferred accounts and Uniform Gifts to Minors Accounts. Municipal zeros have become *the* security for these purposes following tax reform, and their usefulness is so comprehensive for these accounts that we've devoted later chapters to them.

In short, don't base investment decisions exclusively upon your present income and tax situation. Zero coupon municipals purchased today can serve your general and specific portfolio needs well when you take a reasoned look at the future.

SUMMARY

Zero coupon municipal bonds can be very advantageous to all types of investors, not merely the highest taxed. By understanding the importance of quality, call provisions, interest backing, and tax consequence, you can maximize the advantages of these securities.

The outright advantage of municipal zeros is that their accreted interest is exempt from federal income tax. But in the environment investors face as the tax reform of 1986 progresses, municipal zeros are likely to become the foremost type of security in their portfolios. Changed tax brackets and definitions of taxable income have made municipal zeros more attractive because investors are now paying more in federal income tax and can expect to pay even more in the future. Further, so many favored investments have been damaged by changed tax laws that municipal zeros have become the logical replacement for them. Moreover, the behavior of many securities markets has made investors so leery that the predictable accumulations of zeros are a comforting harbor against uncertainty.

Whatever your needs or preferences, zero coupon municipal bonds can be wise additions to your portfolio. Either by themselves or as companions to other types of zero coupon securities, municipal zeros can add balance, dimension, and profits to your investment program.

CHAPTER 5

CONVERTIBLE ZERO COUPON BONDS

Most investors have heard of conventional convertible securities, usually corporate debentures or preferred stocks that can be swapped for another security, most often the common stock of the issuer. By this time it shouldn't surprise you that some corporate zeros have also added a conversion feature to their appeal. As an investor in corporate convertible zeros, you have the option of trading in the bond for the stock.

You also may have heard that EE Savings Bonds can be exchanged for HH Savings Bonds that pay semiannual checks. By exchanging one type of savings bond for another, you can convert accreted interest into an equivalent par value of a current income bond.

What may surprise you, however, is that some types of municipal zeros are now available with a conversion feature that automatically turns them into coupon-paying bonds.

In short, these types of zeros give you the assured accumulations that all zeros offer plus the flexibility to take a position in an equity investment or a current income investment.

CONVERTIBLE MUNICIPAL ZEROS

Convertible municipals are zero coupon bonds that convert into income bonds 10 to 12 years after issue. Consequently, they feature a decade or so of capital growth followed by a decade of current income. This is an ideal investment for combining federally untaxed compounding with federally untaxed coupon income.

To study an example of municipal zero convertibles, let's consider one of the first, those of the Broward County Florida Housing Finance Authority, issued in July 1987. Since these precedent-setting bonds came out, virtually every other convertible municipal has adopted nearly identical features.

The Broward convertible municipals are zero coupon bonds earning interest as the difference between price paid (about $320 per bond when they were issued) and par value of $1,000. Beginning in mid-1997, however, they convert to coupon-paying bonds maturing in 2007 and paying a 10 percent coupon yield ($100 per bond).

In other words, $3,200 invested grows to $10,000 in 1997, a federally untaxed gain of about $6,800 on a yield-to-conversion of 10 percent. From 1997 until 2007, these bonds will pay $1,000 in federally untaxed annual interest—$10,000 over 10 years. In 2007 when the bonds mature, you receive the $10,000 par value to spend or to reinvest. You started out with $3,200 and ended up with $20,000 federally untaxed.

Additionally, convertible municipals might offer further capital growth when they convert to current income bonds. Like all coupon-paying bonds, their prices will increase if their coupon yields are greater then general economywide yields on income investments. For example, the Broward bonds will pay $100, a 10 percent coupon yield, starting in 1997. If economywide rates of interest are generally lower than 10 percent while the Browards are paying coupon income, their prices will rise above $1,000 par value.

Like derivative Treasury zeros, convertible municipals are sold under several names—GAINS (Growth and Income Securities), PACS (Principal Appreciation Conversion Securities), FIGS (Further Income and Growth Securities), TEDIS (Tax-Exempt Discount and Income Securities), and BIGS (Bond Income and Growth Securities)—but they're all fundamentally the same. As long as you understand the basic concept underlying convertible municipal zeros and can ask the pertinent questions about quality and backing outlined in Chapter 4, it doesn't matter what they're called.

Advantages and Disadvantages

It should be easy to see why convertible municipal zeros are attractive investments. Apart from their built-in growth and income, they're safe, predictable, and profitable in addition to being federally untaxed. Consequently, they may be the optimum investment of their type, and they're excellent for investors seeking a period of growth followed by a period of income presented in a single security. All of the present convertible municipals are investment-grade obligations rated A or better, so you can invest with greater confidence against default.

In order to profit from the advantages of municipal convertibles, you have to accept two possible disadvantages. Some convertible municipals are callable before conversion, so you have to ask about yield-to-call as well as yield-to-conversion, although most convertibles have excellent call protection. Also, convertibles fluctuate in price like any publicly traded instrument. If you sell them before maturity, a capital loss is possible, but then so is a capital gain.

Although exempt from federal taxation throughout their lives, municipal convertibles might be subject to state tax where you live. While the convertible is a zero coupon bond, some states expect you to declare accreted interest yearly, whereas others permit you to postpone tax until the bond converts to a current-income bond. When the bond starts paying coupon interest, your state may tax that interest as current income. However, some states don't tax interest on their own securities even if they tax interest on bonds from other states. Ask your broker about tax on municipal convertibles where you live.

Investment Appeal of Convertible Municipals

Municipal convertibles fit the key purpose of retirement-anticipation investments because they offer compounding now and income later. In this respect, their closest investment rival is an ordinary annuity. So let's compare convertibles with annuities:

1. Convertibles are *exempt* from federal tax, whereas annuities merely *defer* tax.
2. Convertibles automatically become income-producing investments, but you have to arrange a payment schedule with the annuity sponsor.
3. Brokerages maintain markets in convertibles, so you can sell them at any time, but if you redeem an annuity before you're $59\frac{1}{2}$ years old, you pay federal tax penalties.
4. Convertibles pay highly predictable returns,whereas the per-

formance of an annuity depends upon the sagacity of investment managers.
5. When your convertible municipal bond ceases coupon payments upon maturity, you can reinvest the par value. An
annuity amortizes to nothing.

However, you don't have to be 50 to 55 years old before convertible municipals can be useful to you, nor must you regard them
only as substitutes for an annuity. They're excellent for investors
of any age, and their federally untaxed coupon yield is competitive with long-term municipals. These are particularly attractive
features for investors who might be interested in early retirement.
Conventional retirement-anticipation investments can't be converted
to current income without tax penalties before you're $59\frac{1}{2}$ years old.
Therefore, if you're planning to retire before age 60, penalties cut
into your retirement income. This isn't the case with convertible
municipals; their payments aren't subject to arbitrary rules about the
age of the recipient. Further, convertible municipals are an excellent
response to a new reality in today's tax and investment climate: the
likelihood that your tax bracket won't decline when you retire.

Until 1986, financial planners routinely assumed your tax bracket
would decline when you reached age 65 as a result of special tax
breaks for the elderly and the generally reduced income that the
elderly receive after they cease working full time. The Tax Reform
Act of 1986 removed many of the tax favors that retired persons
enjoyed, thereby rendering more retirement income fully and partially
taxable. Also, many of today's workers have long participated in
employer investment programs and have undertaken other retirement
investments, such as IRAs, that produce greater income when they do
retire. Coupled with new tax laws that broaden the base of taxable
retirement income, it's been remarkably the case that distributions
from retirement accounts keep retirees in essentially the same brackets
as when they were working. Therefore, federally untaxed municipal
bond income provides as many after-tax advantages as for workers
in their mid-50s, typically the peak of their income and tax years.

Generally speaking, there's no minimum purchase amount
required for investment in convertible municipals, although most brokerages expect you to buy at least $10,000 face value of any munic-
ipal bond and some will require a minimum of $25,000 face value.

And that's face value, not cash outlay. At their modest prices, convertibles are easily affordable, even for very large face values. Their current low cost and formidable advantages in the future are a powerful combination of inducements.

If a minimum investment of $3,000 or $5,000 does present a problem, however, there's a cheaper and more accessible type of convertible zero: your old acquaintance, the EE Savings Bond. It can be a useful retirement-anticipation investment as well as an important vehicle for preretirement.

EE SAVINGS BONDS AND HH SAVINGS BONDS

Although EE bonds pay accreted interest like all zeros, they can be exchanged for HH Savings Bonds paying coupon interest. By exchanging EE for HH bonds, you can have capital growth followed by current income in a particularly tax-advantaged investment.

Like conventional corporate or municipal bonds, HH bonds make semiannual payments until the bond matures 10 years after purchase. HH bonds issued after November 1986 pay 6 percent coupon interest based on par values of $500, $1,000, $5,000, and $10,000. A $10,000 HH bond, for instance, will pay $600 in twice-yearly checks of $300.

Even if you redeem an HH bond before maturity, it will never be worth less than par value, and its capital stability is a major advantage of HH bonds over all other corporate, municipal, or government bonds.

To convert EE bonds for HH bonds, you have to bundle up all of your EE bonds and deliver them to a Federal Reserve Bank or branch or to the Bureau of the Public Debt in Washington, D.C. 20226 or in Parkersburg, West Virginia 26101. When you convert EE bonds for HH bonds, the EEs must be at least six months old and must have accreted to at least $500, the minimum par value for HH bonds.

But here's a special feature: if you convert EE bonds for HH bonds, you need not declare the accreted EE bond interest until you redeem the HH bond or it matures. This special tax-deferral feature means you can defer taxes on your EE bonds for 22 years. Coupon interest paid by the HH is federally taxable, but it isn't taxable by a state or local government, and that's a better deal than your IRA offers.

Converting EE Bonds to HH Bonds

Let's say you expect to retire in 12 years and that you have $5,000 to invest. Here's what you can do.

Buy a $10,000 EE bond and elect to defer interest. Put the bond in a drawer or safety deposit box until it matures in 12 years.

On that date, your initial $5,000 investment will have grown to at least $10,000 if your EE bond paid only the minimum 6 percent interest. If average yields on five-year Treasuries exceeded 6 percent during your holding period, your EE bonds will have grown to more than $10,000 and will be convertible for HH bonds of greater par value.

Convert the EE bond to HH bond in the manner described earlier. By converting, you continue to defer tax on the accreted EE bond interest unless you elect to pay the tax on accreted interest during the year of conversion.

Your $10,000 HH bond will pay $600 interest yearly ($300 every six months) for 10 years. Again, remember that coupon interest from the HH bond is federally taxable, but it is exempt from state and local taxes; that's a particular advantage if you live in a state with burdensome taxes.

Draw interest on your HH bond for 12 years. When the bond finally matures, you must declare all accreted EE bond interest as federally taxable if you have elected to defer it earlier. However, you can reinvest the par value of your HH bonds for continuing returns.

Each individual investor can purchase $30,000 face value of EE bonds each year, but you can register the bonds in multiple ownership to maximize your $30,000 threshold. That is, you can buy $30,000 face value (initial investment of $15,000), your spouse can buy $30,000 face value, and the two of you can register another $30,000 face value in joint ownership. And you can do this *each year* if you can afford to. There is no limit on the exchange of EE bonds for HH bonds; you can acquire as many HH bonds as you have EE bonds to convert.

This strategy with savings bonds also allows you to enjoy early retirement without tax penalties attendant to other retirement investments. If your goal is to accumulate a source of unpenalized retirement income while waiting for a formal retirement program to kick in at age 60 or 65, savings bonds are an excellent investment.

CORPORATE CONVERTIBLE ZEROS

Late 1985 saw the advent of a few zero coupon corporate debentures that offer conversion into stock of the issuing corporation just like the conventional coupon-paying corporate convertible. Just as municipal zeros appeal to investors who like the interest accretion now and current income later, corporate convertible zeros appeal to investors who like to couple the growth possibilities of an equity-equivalent with the advantages of zeros. Such investors are usually long term in their orientation, although, of course, corporate convertible zeros can be played for aggressive gains like any other long-running zero, whether corporate, municipal, or derivative.

Apart from this, they offer a number of attractions:

1. They offer the standard advantages of zeros—low price, known accumulations, fixed reinvestment returns, a defined time horizon.
2. They offer the prospect of price appreciation not only from declines in interest rates but also from appreciation of the underlying stock.
3 Many corporate convertible zeros have "put features," which entitle you to sell the bond back to the issuer at a specified price after a specified date. Put features, which are also available on some zero coupon and conventional municipal bonds, minimize your downside risk.
4. If you convert your corporate convertible zero into stock of the issuing corporation, you may receive some dividend income from the shares of stock you received from converting the zero.

Features of Corporate Convertibles

There are several key terms you should be familiar with if you're considering corporate convertible zeros. Of course, all the terms we've covered with reference to zero coupon investments generally apply to corporate zero convertibles: *yield to maturity, quality rating, par value, maturity, callability,* and *yield to call.* To these terms you add some special vocabulary relating to conversion features.

Conversion ratio is the number of shares you receive when you trade the corporate convertible zero into stock (either common or preferred stock, depending upon the issuing corporation). This figure is revealed in the bond covenant or prospectus. It's important because it tells you how many shares of stock you'll receive if you convert the bond to shares.

Stock price at conversion is the purchase price of the convertible corporate zero divided by the conversion ratio. For instance, if you purchased the corporate convertible for $200 and the conversion ratio is 5, the effective purchase price of the underlying stock is about $40. This figure is important because it shows how much the stock will have to appreciate before it is advantageous to convert the zero into stock.

Conversion Value is the current market value of the number of shares you can receive by converting the zero into stock. To find conversion value, multiply the conversion ratio by the current stock price. For example, if the conversion ratio is 10 and the stock is selling at $20 per share, the conversion value is $200. This figure is important because it tells you how much the bond is worth today, when you're buying the bond, as measured by the price of the stock it's convertible into

Examples of Corporate Convertibles

Let's put these terms to work in an actual example and see how you would use them. In late 1985, Merrill Lynch underwrote five corporate convertible zeros under the trade name LYONS (Liquid Yield Option Notes). One issue was from Waste Management, the Illinois-based international disposer of toxic materials. At issue, Waste Management's LYONS sold for $287.50, carried an A rating, and matured in 20 years at par of $1,000. Its LYONS yielded 8.36 percent to maturity and carried a conversion ratio of 4.36 shares of Waste Management stock, then priced at $60.50 per share.

Our first task is to analyze the zero as a bond. We note that its yield is slightly below that available from CATS and TIGRs of 20-year maturity. But you would expect this to be the case, because the corporate convertible zero offers the potential for appreciation from the underlying stock The sacrifice in yield is the economic cost for the conversion feature, so let's look at this bond with reference to its stock.

As noted, the conversion ratio was 4.36 shares With the bond selling at $287.50, the stock price at conversion was $65.94 (purchase price divided by conversion ratio).

With the common stock of Waste Management selling at $60.50 per share when you bought the convertible corporate zero, you note that you're paying a premium of $5.44 per share for the 4.36 shares of stock you're entitled to if you convert the bond. Therefore, the common stock of Waste Management must approach $66 before it's advantageous to convert the zero to stock.

Even though this may seem to be a disadvantage, you at least know that you're guaranteed ownership of the common stock at a fixed price. Therefore, if Waste Management common stock ever exceeds $66 per share, you have the option of "buying" below market price simply by exercising the conversion privilege. The disadvantage then becomes an advantage—and a source of future gain from the zero.

(By the way, to exercise conversion privileges, you follow the directions on the bond certificate. Those directions will probably tell you to notify the appropriate official of the corporation, usually the corporate secretary, and/or the corporation's transfer agent, which is usually a major bank.)

To estimate that potential for gain, you look at the conversion value (the conversion ratio times current market price of the underlying stock). We multiply 4.36 times the current market price of $60.50 for the stock and derive $263.78. In other words, examining the zero as a stock-equivalent, it's worth $263.78.

Again, there wouldn't seem much reason to buy the LYON instead of buying the stock outright. If you entered the market and bought 4.36 shares of Waste Management stock (actually, you can't buy fractional shares), you would only pay $263.78. If you bought the zero, which is convertible into 4.36 shares, you would pay $287.50. Why pay the extra money? Because the zero appreciates with the underlying stock *and* it retains its value as a zero.

To pick an extreme illustration, say the price of Waste Management stock falls to $1 per share at the end of 20 years, when the zero matures. If you'd bought 4.36 shares of stock, you'd have an investment worth $4.36. The zero would be worth $1,000. In fact, in order to produce the $1,000 that the zero will produce at maturity, the 4.36 shares of stock would have to appreciate to $229.36 apiece.

That's not likely to happen. But even if it does, your zero is convertible into 4.36 shares. The zero will appreciate in price right alongside the 4.36 shares. Moreover, don't forget that the zero will produce capital gains when interest rates fall, regardless of what happens to the stock price. Whether the zero is worth more as a bond or as a stock-equivalent is of little concern to the owner of the zero, because it combines the advantages of stock ownership and zero ownership.

Disadvantages of Corporate Convertibles

Every investment has disadvantages, and so do corporate zeros. Let's examine a few.

1. There are few corporate zeros in existence. These investments are attractive to issuers as well as to buyers, however, so perhaps their numbers will increase.
2. Corporate convertible zeros are potentially more volatile than other zeros. They're subject to the same market fluctuations as other zeros when interest rates change, producing capital losses when rates fall. This is a particular disadvantage with corporate zeros because all of them are currently long-term zeros.
3. Corporate zeros are backed only by the profitability of the issuer, so their prices will fluctuate with the fortunes of the issuing corporations in addition to fluctuating with the changes in interest rates.
4. Unless you buy them for an IRA or Keogh, they generate current tax liability on phantom interest, as do most zeros held outside tax-deferred accounts.

SUMMARY

However you add it up, convertible zeros extend the usefulness and profitability of zero coupon investments generally.

By combining the capital accumulation feature for which zeros are best known with the extra advantage of current income, convertible municipal zeros offer an attractive inducement to consider further the advantages that this singular investment medium provides.

The ordinary EE Savings Bond continues to prove its usefulness as one of the original zero coupon investments. To all of its advantages you saw in Chapter 3, you now must add the advantage of being convertible into an income-producing bond exempt from state and local tax and underpinned by the U.S. government.

The income-convertibility of municipal convertibles and of EE Savings Bonds, plus the capital growth possibilities of corporate convertibles, allows you to assemble a considerable number of advantages in a portfolio of zero coupon investments.

CHAPTER 6

INDIRECT INVESTMENT
IN ZERO COUPON FUNDS

Advantageous as zeros are, you might lack the time, inclination, or capital to purchase them directly—that is, to phone up brokers and place an order for your account. What's more, if you do prefer to invest directly in zeros, you don't always have the capital to invest when attractive issues are released, or maybe when you have the money, there isn't a zero that appeals to you. In short, when the market is ready, maybe you're not, and when you're ready, maybe the market isn't. One solution is to invest indirectly in zeros by subscribing to zero coupon bond funds.

Like customary mutual funds, zero funds assemble money from many investors and buy zeros for all subscribers in the fund. You own shares in the fund—or, to express the situation more conveniently than accurately, you own stock in bonds.

ZERO COUPON BOND FUNDS

The zero fund most attractive to zero coupon investors is a *target fund*, which is slightly different from a customary mutual fund. Conventional bond funds operate indefinitely, constantly buying and trading bonds in their portfolios, adding and deleting securities according to market conditions. Conventional bond funds have a *weighted average maturity*, meaning that they might hold bonds maturing from this year to many years from now. The average maturity is the arithmetic mean maturity of all bonds in the fund, and it is weighted to reflect the emphasis on a particular year of maturity in the fund.

Zero target funds do not operate indefinitely, nor do they have average maturities. Fund managers hold bonds maturing in an identified year, and they offer several discrete portfolios within the overall fund. When bonds in a particular portfolio year mature, that portfolio terminates, sends distributions to shareholders, and that's that. Zero target fund portfolios are identified by year of maturity. For instance, say you have a target fund with five portfolios: 1990, 1995, 2000, 2005, and 2010. You invest in each portfolio as a separate investment, and every bond in each portfolio matures during the indicated year.

Advantages of Zero Target Funds

Zero target funds are advantageous for several reasons. They offer all the advantages of conventional mutual funds. Professional managers select bonds, maintain paperwork, send you account records, redeem shares if you sell, offer switch privileges among funds, and permit you to make additional investments in the fund after you've opened the account. Portfolios in zero target funds don't fluctuate indefinitely in value, as conventional bond funds do. Because bonds mature in an identified year, each portfolio within the fund has a terminal value, and as that year approaches, the net asset value of your investment stabilizes. And, most important for investors in zeros, you can select a zero target fund portfolio as you would select a single bond.

Let's say you're interested in intermediate-term zeros. You can enroll in a zero target fund and choose the portfolio of zeros maturing in 1995. You can also make subsequent contributions. In 1995 the fund closes, and you can reevaluate your needs. You can reinvest in a portfolio with a later maturity, or cash in your holdings. Most zero target funds invest only in zeros derived from Treasury securities, so your money is safe against default. Perhaps someday zero target funds will offer corporate zeros, further expanding the choices open to you.

As with most mutual funds, your purchase price is the fund's net asset value (market value of the fund's securities divided by the number of shares). Most zero funds have no sales charge, but some have yearly account fees. The minimum initial investment for most zero funds is $1,000 ($250 to $500 for Individual Retirement Accounts), and the minimum for subsequent investments is usually

$100. Low minimums for subsequent investment allow you to take advantage of any investor's most formidable investment ally—dollar cost averaging.

Dollar Cost Averaging

Dollar cost averaging is a simple procedure that requires investing a fixed amount at a fixed interval in a zero fund portfolio. To illustrate dollar cost averaging, let's assume that you buy shares of a zero fund portfolio in amounts of $100 each month. Six months from now, your purchase record might resemble this:

Month	Net Asset Value	Shares Purchased	Portfolio Value
Jan	$10 per share	10	$100
Feb	$ 8	12.5	$180
Mar	$ 9	11.111	$302.50
Apr	$10	10	$436.11
May	$11	9.091	$579.72
Jun	$12	8.333	$732.42

You ended the period with a portfolio value of $732.42 (61.035 total shares times $12 per share on the closing date) on an investment of $600. You achieved that gain because dollar cost averaging buys more shares when net asset values are lower and fewer shares when they're higher.

Dollar cost averaging is especially useful for zero funds because funds permit you to buy fractional shares, whereas you can't buy part of a zero if you purchase it directly. Once you've decided to invest in zero funds, dollar cost averaging eliminates timing decisions. You automatically profit from buying more shares of a zero fund when its net asset value is depressed.

However, dollar cost averaging doesn't assure continual gains, because net asset values fluctuate. Note February: Two months into dollar-costing, you had placed $200 into a zero fund valued at $180 (22.5 shares at $8 per share). Had you redeemed the shares, you would have lost 10 percent of your investment. By continuing to dollar cost, you bought more shares at net asset values of $8 and

$9 and benefited when net asset values improved because you were holding more shares.

Zero funds also produce taxation on phantom interest, but again, many investors don't find that a disadvantage. Reinvested interest on *all* bond funds (excluding municipal bond funds) is federally taxable, and essentially interest *is* continually reinvested with your zero fund. Also, remember what we said earlier: too often, we don't let coupon interest compound; we spend it right away, and we end up merely getting par value back. We pay taxes on that dissipated interest, too. So there may be a real advantage to zero funds despite taxation on phantom income, and their situation isn't any worse than the norm.

If you dislike paying taxes on interest you haven't actually frittered away, you have two alternatives. First, invest your IRA or Keogh in zero funds to compound untaxed, or use zero funds for Uniform Gifts to Minors Accounts, for which taxable phantom interest is negligible. If you buy zeros for your IRA, dollar cost averaging is a disciplined way to set aside your maximum yearly contribution, and dollar costing UGMAs is a convenient way to attend to your children's future. Second, invest in zero funds that hold federally tax-exempt zero coupon municipal securities.

TAX-EXEMPT SECURITIES TRUSTS

Familiar to most investors, the two most familiar types of indirect investments offering municipal securities are the municipal bond fund and the municipal securities trust. For people seeking indirect investment in municipal zeros, however, these two familiar vehicles aren't useful. Municipal bond mutual funds don't invest in zeros, and rarely will municipal securities trusts mix zeros with coupon-paying municipals. But investing in a portfolio of zero coupon municipals is possible through an investment vehicle similar to a mutual fund and to a municipal securities trust. It's called a *tax-exempt securities trust*.

This trust is similar to a municipal bond mutual fund in that it takes money from many investors and purchases a portfolio of municipal bonds in which each investor owns a part (as we noted, however, municipal bond funds buy only coupon-paying municipals).

That, too, is the principle behind the conventional municipal securities trust, which also invests in coupon-paying municipal bonds.

Like the municipal securities trust, the tax-exempt securities trust is usually an unmanaged portfolio. Whereas mutual bond fund managers will constantly add and delete securities from their fund's holdings, managers of municipal securities trusts and tax-exempt securities trusts operate a fixed portfolio. Unless market conditions change drastically or an issue within the trust deteriorates substantially in its creditworthiness, managers of a municipal trust won't alter the composition of the trust's holdings.

Managers of tax-exempt securities trusts have discovered the popularity of zero coupon municipals and have also discovered that the two best known forms of indirect municipal investment haven't capitalized on the popularity of zeros. Accordingly, these managers have created portfolios of municipal zeros and offered them to investors who don't want to buy municipals directly.

With zero coupon municipals, accreted interest is federally untaxed, and tax-exempt securities trusts holding municipal zeros also escape federal tax. State tax may or may not apply in your state, and infrequent capital gains will be fully taxed. Tax-exempt securities trusts pass on the tax advantages and the investment advantages of the trust to you. In addition, they offer the advantages associated with professional management and recordkeeping services.

The chief disadvantage is that tax-exempt securities trusts aren't target funds, so they don't have precise maturities and interest rates. The trust will terminate at some distant point, but not all of its zeros mature in the same year. Tax-exempt securities trusts hold several series of maturities, and the whole portfolio won't mature simultaneously. We've cited maturity as an important criterion in selecting municipal zeros. Thus, from the point of view of known maturity, tax-exempt securities trusts are slightly disadvantaged.

As an investor in a tax-exempt securities trust, you buy units in a comprehensive portfolio, and you'll be quoted a yield to average maturity. The minimum purchase is usually 5 or 10 units, requiring an initial investment of $5,000 to $10,000. Most tax-exempt securities trusts are diversified with municipal zeros from many states, adding safety should any issue default.

Dollar cost averaging usually isn't possible with tax-exempt securities trusts. They don't usually permit subsequent investments because the portfolio is fixed. Some do, but, unlike target funds, trusts generally won't accept subsequent deposits and buy more bonds. You can buy additional units from sponsoring brokerages if they have any in inventory. Otherwise, you can't buy additional units unless another investor will sell them. At worst, you'll have to wait for another series of the trust, and you'll probably not have a long wait.

MONEY MARKET FUNDS

If you're a contemporary American investor, you're probably already investing in a zero coupon fund without knowing it. In Chapter 3, where we covered original issue corporate zeros, we mentioned several types of investments—specifically, T-bills, commercial paper, repurchase agreements, and international letters of credit—that generally are too high-priced for most individual investors. These vehicles are high-quality, short-term obligations maturing within a few days to less than a year, and they're generally offered by major financial institutions and corporations. Nearly all conventional money funds are populated almost exclusively by these zero coupon investments.

Even if these investments are too rich for your wallet, they're purchased in sizable quantity by managers of money market funds, and they're available to you as an indirect investor who subscribes to the fund. For as little as $1,000 and often less, you can become part owner of a portfolio of these investments and add the advantages of very short-term zeros to your holdings.

The chief advantage to money funds is their constant net asset value. Because the zeros in a money fund mature so quickly, the net asset value of your fund remains at a constant $1. There's no capital fluctuation, which is a key disadvantage of zeros for some investors. Therefore, they're excellent savings vehicles and are also useful as a temporary parking lot for cash awaiting investment elsewhere.

In addition, money funds pay market-level returns that have varied between 5 and 20 percent in the recent past. Their prominence as investments that keep pace with inflation makes them especially useful, as we'll discuss later, and their stable net asset value also makes them useful for recessions.

Moreover, money market funds offer instant liquidity without commissions in any economic environment. Most funds feature checking privileges that permit you to cash your holdings in a familiar manner, and those few money funds that don't offer checking will have telephone redemption features.

There are three types of money funds. The first invests exclusively in T-bills and other government paper for maximum security. The second invests in T-bills and corporate paper for maximum returns. The third invests in short-term municipal paper for federally untaxed returns, a major advantage for reducing your federal tax burden.

You can subscribe to a money market fund through any mutual fund family, a bank or S&L, and virtually any full-service or discount brokerage. Although not commonly thought of as a zero coupon fund, that's exactly what money market funds are. If you're already investing in a money market fund, you should have greater confidence to invest in other types of zero coupon funds. If you're one of the few investors who aren't conversant with money market funds, consult *Starting Small Investing Smart,* also written by your author.

SUMMARY

Zero coupon funds offer many of the advantages of direct investment in zeros. They can serve a range of portfolio strategies and time horizons while minimizing your investment. Zero funds make capital markets more accessible for less capitalized investors, and they definitely deserve consideration as part of your total holdings of zeros.

CHAPTER 7

NEW DIRECTIONS AND DEVELOPMENTS IN ZERO COUPON INVESTMENTS

There are many types of zero coupon investments, and many were around for decades before innovative brokerage firms severed the principal and interest certificates from Treasury bonds to create derivative zero coupon bonds. Since then, however, zero coupon products have sprouted distinctive features, some borrowed from old-fashioned zeros like EE Savings Bonds, others adapted from similar investments like convertible corporate debentures, and a few with advantages created by special tax circumstances. Financial markets are expanding the advantages of zeros by creating and proposing new zero products that are potentially more flexible and popular than zeros are now.

ZEROS FROM GOVERNMENTAL AGENCIES

Although Treasury-backed zeros created by stripping coupons and interest from conventional Treasury securities are the best known, Treasury agency securities are proliferating in number. In some cases, these government agency zeros are backed by a credit pledge from Uncle Sam. In other cases, the securities are presumed, rightly or wrongly, to carry that pledge. For either reason, agency zeros are rated AAA.

At present, you can buy zeros issued by the World Bank, the Student Loan Marketing Association, the Government National Mortgage Association, the Federal National Mortgage Association, Tennessee Valley Authority, Chattanooga Valley Authority, and the Federal Farm Credit System, to name only a few.

One type of zero that's been especially controversial is issued by Financing Corporation. Called FICOs, these zeros are issued by a congressionally-mandated organization and their purpose is to assist—some would say "bail out"—the savings and loan industry. Several billion dollars in par value of FICOs are now outstanding in public markets, and the problem seems to be that multiple billions of dollars more might be needed to assure the effective purpose of Financing Corporation.

The magnitude of sums involved has called attention to the growing number of assurances that the federal government is providing to agency securities at a time when the federal government's conventional debt is already a major concern. The warnings and recriminations that characterize these discussions have produced more heat than light and more concerns than conclusions. Neither the AAA rating nor the market for agency zeros has been diminished.

All of the above considerations aside, you should appreciate this expanded assortment of high-quality zero coupon issues for a potential place in your portfolio. Prices are often slightly lower and yields slightly higher for agency zeros, making them particularly attractive in light of their presumed or actual backing by the Treasury.

ZERO COUPON FUNDS COUPLED WITH COMMODITIES

Late in 1985, several brokerage houses designed a zero fund that mates the capital assurance features of zeros with aggressive investments in commodities and futures, perhaps the most speculative of all investment vehicles. This selected type of zero fund offers the chance for aggressive gains through commodities trading *and* assures investors who hold the fund until maturity that they'll at least get their original investment back. Consequently, it provides a form of aggressive investment that virtually eliminates the prospect of total capital loss so prevalent with outright commodities trading or investment in commodity funds.

These funds usually require you to invest at least $5,000 for five to seven years ($2,000 for an IRA). The managers take one third to two thirds of your investment and place the money in Treasury zeros. With the present levels of interest rates, this portion of the investment will equal the amount of your original investment by the time the fund matures. The remaining portion of your investment is placed into futures and commodities contracts—currencies and financial futures, metals, agricultural futures, energy futures, stock indices, and whatever else looks promising—in an attempt to produce extraordinary gains.

Apart from assurance that you won't go absolutely broke (in fact, you should receive all of your original capital back if you stay in the fund until it terminates), you have diversification within a portfolio of commodities and futures investments and the advantage of professional managers investing on your behalf in these intensely volatile markets.

These funds offer an excellent way to participate in the capital accumulation features of zeros and the exponential gains of futures trading. In addition, other advantages of the fund include no management fee (an incentive fee will apply on a percentage of profits, and the broker from whom you bought the fund will receive a commission), restriction of margin responsibility to the fund managers, and interest paid on cash balances.

If necessary, you can redeem your units in the fund upon appropriate written notification, although you aren't assured of preserving capital or securing an investment gain if you redeem your units before the fund matures.

If you're interested in the aggressive possibilities from this conservatively novel investment, you'll have to meet suitability requirements. You'll have to show net worth of at least $75,000 excluding home and personal possessions or a minimum net worth of $30,000 plus an annual income of at least $30,000. Suitability standards may be higher in some states.

A related type of fund mates zeros with precious metals. Managers place a portion of your investment into zeros and the remainder into bullion, usually gold. You receive the capital appreciation potential of the bullion plus the capital recovery potential of the zeros if nothing happens to the price of gold.

These innovative approaches in creating an aggressive gains investment with minimal downside risk show the exceptional range of possibilities that zeros afford. Even if you aren't interested in this type of zero coupon innovation, you should at least appreciate now how incredibly versatile zeros are and how innovative you can be in using them in many financial circumstances.

SPLIT FUNDING CONCEPT WITH STOCKS

In Part II you'll see how to mate zero coupon securities with common stocks to assure stable and optimum returns from the growth component of your portfolio. Now there are unit investment trusts that will do that for you.

During the past several years, several major brokerage firms have offered trusts that, like the commodity funds, split your investment between stocks and zeros. From the stock component, you receive potential capital gains; from the zero component, you are assured of recovering your initial capital if you stay with the trust until it matures. As a further point that you'll see in Part II, this split funding concept also maximizes returns when stocks don't perform as exceptionally as predicted.

These trusts have varying initial minimum investments and maturities, although $5,000 and five years are common. You can withdraw from the trusts prior to maturity, but in that case you're not assured of a capital gain or of recovering your initial investment. Stock/zero funds offer the conventional advantages of recordkeeping, reinvestment, and professional management that are characteristic of mutual funds. The disadvantage is that you have no voice in your portfolio decisions.

Contact your broker to see if his or her firm offers split funding trusts.

TAX-FREE INTEREST ON EE SAVINGS BONDS?

A few years ago, the U.S. Treasury Department solicited from the general public recommendations on improving the appeal of EE Savings Bonds. Among the proposals received was one that suggested exempting the first $1,000 of federally taxable EE bond accreted interest. The Treasury did not accept the recommendation, but similar proposals have come forth since.

As this book was going to press, Senator Ted Kennedy proposed that an amount of EE bond interest be exempted from federal tax if investors could demonstrate that the accreted interest was used to pay tuition. A related circumstance arose from the presidential campaign of George Bush, who offered a "modest additional proposal" that would permit some investors to accrue federally untaxed sums from conventional savings accounts for a period of five years. If anything further happens with his suggestion, EE Savings Bonds could become a logical security for implementing it.

It is clear that the U.S. national debt is a subject of increasing worry in world financial markets. Savings bonds, which pay less interest than other Treasury obligations, could help lower the cost of financing the federal debt if they're made more attractive to personal investors. EE bonds already offer many inducements, including ease of purchase and affordability in many denominations, and it's not inconceivable that they could become greater tools of financial policy if the Treasury Department takes them more seriously. Keep your eye on them in the future.

MUNICIPAL COLLEGE BONDS

In 1988, several states floated issues of zero coupon municipal bonds with a special inducement for parents: accreted interest would be municipally untaxed if it were used to pay college tuition. In some cases, the bonds contained grant provisions that made students eligible for state grants if the bonds were held to maturity. Already federally untaxed, these bonds drew a resonant response from tax-minded and college-minded investors.

Generally known as *college bonds,* this idea has become so popular that new issues of them from other states already are under development. One particular advantage is that parents can hold these zeros in their own names and achieve the substantial tax advantages of an investment earmarked for children. College bonds are a substantial extension of the usefulness of zero coupon municipal bonds. Take advantage of them as an integral part of tuition planning for your children.

FOREIGN ZEROS

Although there hasn't been large volume sponsorship of zero coupon securities from the international community, that won't be the case indefinitely. With zero coupon investments already popular with Americans, it's likely that foreign issuers will tap the enthusiasm. Some issuers already have. Australia, New Zealand, Sweden, Israel, and Canada have retailed full faith and credit zero coupon securities in U.S. markets. In addition, some countries issue the equivalent of their own EE Savings Bonds that can be owned by their citizens who live abroad even though other nationalities can't buy them.

In most cases, these foreign zeros are denominated in U.S. dollars, removing the possibility of currency translation losses. In other cases, the zeros are denominated in the currency of the issuer. As the American dollar loses its robustness in foreign exchange, assets denominated in foreign currencies become more popular for American investors. Of course, if the dollar appreciates against those currencies, the zeros' payments of accreted interest will be less valuable. Whatever the case, international zeros are an excellent way to diversify your portfolio globally. At present, foreign zeros retailed in the U.S. are rated AAA.

In late 1988 the government of Israel floated an issue of its own bonds, backed 90 percent by a pledge of assurance from the U.S. government. The remaining portion of the issue was collateralized by U.S. Treasury securities. In effect, these are foreign bonds denominated in dollars, which can call upon the U.S. government for payment of principal and interest if Israel defaults. This opportunity for a foreign investment was well received by U.S. investors, although the question arose as to why the U.S. government was pledging to support the bonds of another nation.

THIRD WORLD DEBT

In 1987 and 1988, the debt "crisis" of lesser developed nations precipitated a response in the form of zero coupon bonds. Owners of the debt, generally large U.S. banks, issued zero coupon bonds that were "collateralized" by the interest and principal promises of the outstanding loans. Investors who bought the zeros presumably will be paid as the loan proceeds are repaid.

The question, of course, is what will happen to the zeros if the loans aren't repaid? Some parties have argued that the issuing banks themselves will be responsible for their zeros, and others have suggested that the burden of default might be passed on to the U.S. taxpayer because the issuing banks are FDIC insured.

BABY BOND ZEROS

Nearly all stripped Treasuries have par values of $1,000, but the Treasury Bond Receipts (TBRs) created in 1982 by E.F. Hutton are an exception. Hutton has since merged with Shearson Lehman Brothers, but its TBRs are still available.

Par values of these zeros are $250, $275, $285, or $475. Their reduced pars mean that purchase prices are even smaller than for CATS or TIGRs with pars of $1,000. Accordingly, they are especially useful for investors with modest amounts to set aside in zeros. The minimum required investment ranges from $500 upward, for which you can purchase two to five bonds. The most distant maturity of TBRs is 2006.

You might want to keep TBRs in mind if you have odd sums in your IRA or Keogh. A few hundred dollars lying around might not be enough to purchase the required lot of CATS or TIGRs, but it will be enough to pick up a few TBRs.

SUMMARY

It's clear that we haven't seen the last of innovations in zero coupon products. Whatever financial markets bring in the years ahead, zero coupon products are sure to gain increasing favor from the investing public—and for many good reasons. With their combinations of profitable features, zeros are here to stay, and with new developments, they're likely to become even more profitable and versatile.

PART 2

MANAGING
ZERO COUPON
INVESTMENTS

A balanced portfolio contains components for savings, current income, capital growth, aggressive gains, and lump sum accumulation. Investors have discovered that zero coupon investments can serve all five of these critical portfolio elements (see Figure II–1).

The base of your financial house comprises short-term zeros like T-bills and money market funds to create a firm foundation. These short-term zeros provide the stability, liquidity, and market-level returns necessary for savings.

The left wall of your financial house represents the current income portion of the portfolio, discussed in Chapter 9. It is erected with convertible municipal zeros, EE Savings Bonds convertible into current income HH bonds, and zeros with serialized maturities to produce spendable cash in hand.

The right wall of your financial house represents the capital growth component of the portfolio. Convertible corporate zeros are located along this wall, where they function as a stock equivalent for capital growth. Zero coupon CDs, intermediate-term zeros from corporations, municipalities, and other sources provide predictable capital growth that often exceeds more customary investments for capital growth.

FIGURE II–1

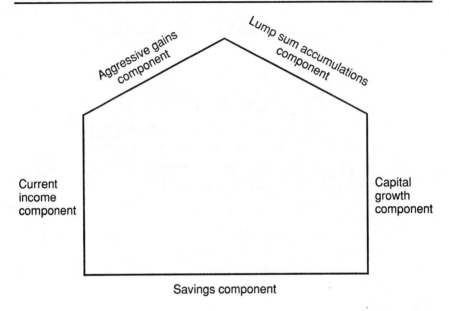

Savings	Income	Capital growth	Aggressive	Lump sum
T-bills	Convertibles	Convertibles	Long-term	IRA/Keogh
Money funds	Serialized zeros	Supporting zeros	Zero/	UGMA
	EE/HH bonds	Zero/Stock units	Commodity	Municipal
			funds	zeros
				Zero funds

The left roof of your financial house represents the aggressive gains component of the portfolio. It contains long-term zeros purchased for short-term gains from changes in interest rates. The **zero/commodity funds** mentioned in Chapter 7 also fit here, where they can produce the above average returns that characterize aggressive investments.

The right roof represents the lump sum component of the portfolio, designed to accommodate anticipated needs for cash in the future—for retirement, for example, or in accumulating funds for children's tuition. With their predictable maturities, yields, and accumulations, many types of zero coupon investments are perfect for the lump sum component

CHAPTER 8

ZERO COUPON INVESTMENTS AND THE SAVINGS COMPONENT

Savings is a specific kind of investment, one that earns market-level returns, fluctuates minimally in price, and is easily converted to cash without excessive costs. With capital stability, liquidity, and minimum commissions as your savings goals, you might think that most zeros aren't suited for the savings component.

Zero coupon CDs are highly stable, but they often bear interest penalties if redeemed before maturity, so they don't provide ready liquidity. EE Savings Bonds are suited for what you might call long-term savings because they're invulnerable to market fluctuations, but they're illiquid before six months and don't pay market-level interest in their early years. Long-term corporate and derivative zeros fluctuate too much in price and aren't capital stable by any means.

But by the time you've read this far, you've learned not to rule out zeros for any portfolio purpose. Two types of zeros are perfect for the savings component of your portfolio because they do exactly what savings are supposed to do. In fact, when most investors speak of savings-type investments, they're talking about U.S. Treasury bills and money market funds, both of which are zero coupon investments. Besides T-bills and money funds, you also can call upon short-term corporate, Treasury, and municipal zeros for the savings component.

U.S. TREASURY BILLS

As we noted in Chapter 2, T-bills are short-term obligations of the U.S. Treasury that sell at discounts below par and mature in 13, 26 or 52 weeks. Brief maturities assure relative capital stability, and as the next best thing to cash they're easily sold if you need the money. Their returns are the measure of market-level returns, so there's no problem in earning what the market will pay. In addition, interest from T-bills is exempt from state and local tax, adding further to the posttax returns from your savings component.

You can buy T-bills from any full-service brokerage firm and from most discount brokerages, and commissions will range from $30 to $100. Most banks and S&Ls will buy bills for you, although their fees often exceed commissions from brokers. If you have a substantial account or a long-standing relationship with a depositary institution, however, it may charge minimal fees to maintain your good will. To buy new issues of T-bills without commissions, submit a noncompetitive tender directly to the U.S. government.

Every week, the Treasury refinances billions of dollars worth of existing T-bills and floats new ones. Major national and international financial institutions, depositaries of all sizes, and well-capitalized private investors submit competitive tenders for these securities. That is, they study markets and interest rate trends and attempt to achieve the highest returns by specifying a price at which they'll purchase T-bills during weekly auctions.

By submitting a noncompetitive tender, however, you inform the Federal Reserve, as agent for the Treasury, that you'll pay the average price and accept the average yield at which the T-bills are auctioned. Although you may receive a decimal lower interest than big-money buyers who study T-bill markets full time, you're almost assured of receiving a T-bill because the Federal Reserve fills noncompetitive tenders first.

Call or write the nearest Federal Reserve Bank or branch, and representatives will mail you complete information about buying T-bills, including forms for executing the transaction. (The forms aren't absolutely necessary. You can write the Federal Reserve a letter, explaining that you want to submit a noncompetitive tender and specifying the date of the auction and the maturity you're interested in buying.)

Mail or hand deliver your letter to the Fed along with a cashier's check for at least $10,000, the minimum purchase price for one bill. T-bills are also sold in increments of $5,000 beyond the minimum, so you can purchase bills for $10,000, $15,000, and so on.

You pay the full par value when you submit your offer. When your offer is accepted, the Federal Reserve will mail you a check for the difference between par value and average purchase price. If, for example, 13-week bills sell for an average of $9,500, you'll receive a check for $500. The check is a return of principal and is untaxed.

Your T-bill will be registered in book entry form on computer tape. You'll receive a confirmation notice indicating the registration number of your bill and its maturity.

The most convenient way to manage your T-bills is to roll them over at the end of each maturity period, automatically buying a new bill of the same maturity when the old one matures. If you intend to roll bills over, so indicate when you buy bills initially. The Federal Reserve, broker, or banking agent will execute your intention as another concompetitive tender when the bill matures. You pay no commissions or fees on T-bill rollovers.

When you purchase the subsequent bill, you will once again receive a check for the difference between par value and average purchase price. However, in this case the check represents interest paid on the preceding T-bill.

The check may be more or less than actual interest received, depending upon the average price of T-bills at the second auction. For example, for the first noncompetitive tender you paid $9,500 for a $10,000 T-bill, and you got back $500, which was a return of capital. When that bill matures, you'll receive $10,000. However, perhaps at the second auction T-bills sell for $9,600—$100 more. When you roll the first T-bill over and use it to buy a second bill, you'll receive a check for $400, but you'll still have received $500 in federally taxable interest. Like any other borrower to whom you loan money, the Treasury will apprise you of interest earned, which makes your recordkeeping easier.

Of course, you don't have to buy T-bills when they're originally issued. You can buy them any time in the open market through brokers and depositaries. In this case, the market will establish the price, not the average price that prevailed when you submitted a noncompetitive tender.

If you hold a T-bill until maturity, your payment will be interest (subject to federal tax but exempt from state and local taxes). But if you sell your T-bill prior to maturity, the difference between your purchase price and sale price will be a capital gain or loss. Interest isn't taxable until the bill matures. Capital gains are taxed and capital losses are declared for the year in which you sold the bill.

Calculating Prices on T-Bills

If you buy T-bills at Federal Reserve auctions, you'll send in a cashier's check for $10,000 (plus even multiples of $5,000). When buying T-bills on public markets, however, market quotations don't specify a price. Instead, dealers buy and sell at a specified rate of return.

For example, suppose while reading the T-bill quotations in *The Wall Street Journal* that you see a bill with the bid discount of 5.66 percent and the asked discount is 5.59 percent of par value. The dealer wants to buy this bill at prices producing a 5.66 percent return and sell this bill at prices producing a 5.59 percent rate of return. This *interest rate spread* is the dealer's profit. Dealers will always want to buy bills at lower prices (higher rates) and sell them at higher prices (lower rates).

Let's assume you want to buy one bill at the asked price and that the bill is 31 days from maturity (count the day of purchase in your calculation). To determine your market price, use this formula:

$$\text{Price} = \text{Par Value} - \frac{(\text{Par Value} \times \text{Asked Discount} \times \text{Number of Days to Maturity})}{360}$$

Figures enter the formula, using the financial year of 360 days rather than the customary calendar of 365 days:

$$\text{Price} = \$10,000 - \frac{(\$10,000 \times .0559 \times 31)}{360}$$

$$\text{Price} = \$10,000 - (\$48.14) = \$9,951.86$$

You'll pay $9,951,86 plus commission to buy this bill. The interest you'll receive upon maturity equals the dollar discount from purchase price. In 31 days, you'll receive $10,000, or $48.14 more than you paid.

MONEY MARKET FUNDS

For the past 20 years, the money market fund has been the preferred savings vehicle of most investors. In reality, money market funds are a special type of zero coupon fund, and they offer market-level returns, liquidity by check, no capital fluctuation, and no commissions or fees. That combination fits perfectly with the needs of the savings component.

Moreover, money market funds don't require a $10,000 minimum investment. Most are available for as little as $500 to $2,000 and you can add to your savings as your finances permit in amounts as little as $1. With their low minimums for initial and subsequent investment, money market funds are the ideal vehicle for serving the savings component of the portfolio with indirect investment in zero coupon bonds.

As an added advantage, you can invest in municipal money funds, which are not federally taxed. You can select money funds that invest only in government obligations for optimum assurance against default. This choice is basically the same as investing directly in T-bills, because government money funds typically hold T-bills as the majority of their portfolios; however, money market payments usually are fully taxable. Finally, you can invest in a conventional money market fund containing corporate securities for the highest return.

Any of these types of money market funds will suit your savings component. What's more, this type of zero coupon bond fund is an excellent parking lot for capital you're waiting to invest elsewhere, and it's also a perfect investment during times of economic uncertainty, as you'll see later.

SHORT-TERM ZEROS AND ZERO FUNDS FOR SAVINGS

Any investment grade corporate, Treasury, or municipal zero with a short-term maturity offers liquidity and relative capital stability. Zeros maturing in under two years will be less volatile than their long-running counterparts, so they have the relative stability needed for savings. Also, public markets make them liquid, although usefulness in the savings component will be diminished by commissions.

Near-term corporate or derivative zeros are possible choices for the savings component, although near-term zeros from funds might be a better choice. The initial investment will be lower than for direct purchase of zeros—certainly lower than for direct purchase of T-bills—and low minimums for subsequent investment are attractive for savers. Commissions are likely to be lower, too.

If direct purchase of zeros or indirect investment in zero funds proves advantageous, following a few guidelines will help make the most of zeros in the savings component.

First, select near-term zeros maturing in the same year. Then, if you do need to sell your zeros for an emergency, you needn't expend time in selling different series of zeros. If you're investing in a zero fund, pick the nearest-term portfolio and contribute to it regularly. If you have to redeem shares, you'll have your money in one place and won't have to execute multiple redemptions.

Second, try to buy and hold your savings zeros with a brokerage firm that maintains its own market. If you must sell before the bonds mature, perhaps you'll escape with smaller commissions than if you bought your zeros in public markets.

Third, if you aren't forced to sell or redeem zeros for an emergency and are able to hold them until maturity, reinvest their proceeds immediately in another series of zeros or in another portfolio of the zero fund.

By following these steps, you can use zeros other than T-bills in the savings component of the portfolio, although the former are preferable for savings.

SUMMARY

T-bills are the original-issue zeros most favorable to savings, because they are stable, liquid, and produce market-level returns. For the investor lacking the cash for a T-bill's high investment minimum, money market funds meet the same objectives, plus they offer checking features and the opportunity for subsequent investment. Other types of short-term zeros, whether purchased directly or through mutual funds, also can be useful in the savings component. Whatever your choices, zeros will meet the objectives and purposes of savings.

CHAPTER 9

ZERO COUPON INVESTMENTS AND THE CURRENT INCOME COMPONENT

The most frequent criticism of zero coupon investments is that they are useless to investors who need or prefer current income investments. Such investors are the retired, who need dividends and interest to supplement pensions, Social Security, and retirement plans, and investors of all ages who prefer current income investments because they can reinvest interest and dividends for compound growth.

You've seen that these criticisms don't hold for two types of zero coupon investments: the convertible municipal bond and EE Savings Bonds convertible into coupon-paying HH bonds. As you're about to learn, although other types of zeros don't pay interest until maturity, zeros can be arranged to produce current income by scheduling maturities carefully. But taking first things first, let's begin our discussion of zeros and the current income component by looking at convertible issues.

CONVERTIBLE MUNICIPAL ZEROS

As we noted in Chapter Five, convertible municipal zeros grow as ordinary zero coupon bonds for a certain period and then automatically become conventional coupon-paying bonds. Because of their predictable growth and predictable period of income payments, convertible zeros are exceedingly useful, perhaps even preferable, alternatives to annuities in retirement planning. Their conversion to income investments is specified in the bond covenant, and you needn't take any action to begin receiving income from these instruments. You do, however, have to plan for periods of capital accumulation and income when purchasing them.

At present, most issues of convertible municipal zeros hold their capital accumulation phase for 10 to 12 years before converting to income investments. Obviously, the easiest way to manage them is to buy them 10 years before you think you'll need their income. If you plan to retire at age 65, go shopping for convertible zeros in your mid to late 50s. Their current income phase should conveniently coincide with the beginning of your retirement.

Bear in mind, however, that you may have different needs for income at different periods of retirement. If, for example, you purchased an annuity, perhaps its income stream coupled with Social Security and pension will be sufficient for your early retirement years. In this case, perhaps you need current income from convertibles at a later stage of your retirement, in which case you can postpone buying convertibles in your preretirement years.

On the other hand, perhaps you'll need greater income early in your retirement, say, if you have children finishing college during your mid-60s, or if you're expecting some other temporary drain on your finances. In this case, you'll want to arrange maximum payments early in your retirement.

Whatever your particular situation, you need to plan your convertible municipal zeros for payments that suit your needs. That means you must assess your sources of retirement income—IRAs, Social Security, personal investments, pensions, rental payments—and determine how your convertibles can best fit with your other sources of income.

EE AND HH SAVINGS BONDS

The same holds true for converting EE Savings Bonds into coupon-paying HH bonds. In Chapter 5, we outlined how this procedure can work to your advantage. You exchange your zero coupon EE bonds (retaining their federal tax deferral if you wish) for HH bonds by mailing them to the Treasury Department or a Federal Reserve Bank or branch. When doing so, however, you must decide the frequency of income you need from HH bonds, because, unlike other Treasury bonds, the date of semiannual interest payments from HH bonds is established on the date of conversion.

If you bought a publicly traded Treasury bond, it would pay interest semiannually on a date established when the bond was issued, regardless of when you purchased it. So if you bought a bond maturing in May of any year, it would pay interest in May and November every year until it matured. A bond maturing in June would pay semiannual interest in June and December. And so on throughout the calendar.

However, when you convert EE bonds to HH bonds, you'll begin receiving coupon interest payments (6 percent of par value) six months from the date of conversion. Your date of conversion establishes the schedule of semiannual interest. If you ship in all your matured EE bonds at once, you'll receive income only twice yearly. But if you convert your EE bonds serially—convert some in January, some in February, and so on—you'll establish a more frequent payment schedule for your HH bonds. Bonds converted in January will pay interest in July and January; in February, August and February; in March, September and March, and so on.

As always, you must assess your needs for current income and arrange conversion of your EE Savings Bonds accordingly. However, you can make the most of scheduling income from zeros by carefully arranging maturities in other ways, and in this case you can take full advantage of the range of zeros available.

ARRANGING CURRENT INCOME BY SERIALIZED MATURITIES

In arranging zeros to provide current income, you rely upon the most convenient characteristic of zeros: their single payment upon maturity. It doesn't matter if the zero is a TIGR, a CD, a municipal or corporate zero, or a zero coupon fund. You can serialize zeros to receive a predictable payment.

The example you're about to examine is an instance of an investor contriving current income by investing a lump sum distribution from an employer. But the same principle holds for managing any distribution, be it a matured IRA, a portfolio of other zeros, a life insurance or estate settlement, or a single payment from an annuity.

Let's say that you retire at age 59 and receive a lump sum distribution from your employee investment plan. Among other alternatives, tax law permits you to place those proceeds into an IRA rollover account. In the rollover, as with standard IRAs, tax is deferred until you accept a payment as fully taxable current income.

In this case, you can take the lump sum distribution and purchase zeros of serialized yearly maturities. As each zero matures, you can accept the proceeds and use them for current income (or reinvestment). We'll use a 10-year term for convenience, although you can arrange any schedule that fits your circumstances, and we'll assume the lump sum distribution is $100,000.

Let's say that you decide to invest 10 increments of approximately $10,000, although, of course, you can arrange any apportionment that you prefer. Your schedule might resemble this, but remember that prices change daily and these are only approximations:

Age	Year	Cost per Zero	Total Outlay	Total Accumulations
60	1	$870	$ 9,570	$ 11,000
61	2	800	9,600	12,000
62	3	735	9,555	13,000
63	4	600	9,600	16,000
64	5	550	9,900	18,000
65	6	490	9,800	20,000
66	7	400	10,000	25,000
67	8	370	9,990	27,000
68	9	350	9,800	28,000
69	10	333	9,990	30,000
Investment Totals			$97,805	$200,000

Although we've not considered commissions, you can see that you not only receive yearly income of the amount indicated at the right but also turn $100,000 into $200,000 without exaggerated market maneuverings. This particular example arranges greater income in later years, but with a little shuffling of money up front you can twist the income schedule any way you prefer. One disadvantage with this arrangement is that you receive income only once yearly when the zeros mature. However, remember that this schedule supplements any other income you may receive.

A schedule of this type lets you see when your investments are maturing and aids your planning. You can prepare it by hand or keep it on file and continually updated in a home computer. For your further convenience, you have a worksheet in the Appendix that you can photocopy for use throughout portfolio planning. You'll also see something resembling this chart in our chapter on zero coupon investments and the lump sum component of the portfolio. It's very useful in helping you maximize the planning certainty of zeros, whether you're planning for income or arranging any other aspect of your portfolio.

The particular advantage of zeros in the current income component of the portfolio is that you can select a variety of zero coupon investments. If there isn't a CAT or TIGR maturing in a given year, select a corporate zero, a zero CD, or a zero bond fund with a compatible maturity. Now that you know the types of zeros available, you can choose among them for your convenience and profit, selecting maturities you need from the range of zeros available.

This example has been of a tax-deferred IRA rollover, but you can use this schedule for any of your zero coupon investments, including savings bonds, municipals, and funds, even though different tax considerations may apply.

Just to illustrate how to fit zeros into the current income component, let's review the portfolio of a real investor, a 62-year-old widow who's just received a life insurance settlement from her late husband's insurance company. In this investor's case, current income from part-time work and other investments is more than adequate for current needs. She plans to work part-time for three years, and she would like to live off the proceeds of investing her insurance settlement. Her late husband's financial advisor has worked out the following arrangement for her. Because we're interested in examining the diversity of zeros in providing current income and not their accumulations, we'll merely list her investments and not report their dollar value or par values.

With this arrangement, our widowed investor will have an assured source of income for the next decade as a supplement to pension, Social Security, and investment income. Because taxes are a minimal consideration in this case, the investor and her advisor

Year	Age	Zero Coupon Investment
1989	65	Money market fund
1990	66	Zero coupon target fund with 1990 maturity
1991	67	Zero coupon CD purchased from a brokerage
1992	68	Derivative zero purchased from a brokerage
1993	69	Derivative zero purchased from a brokerage
1994	70	Derivative zero purchased from a brokerage
1995	71	Zero coupon municipal bond
1996	72	Zero coupon municipal bond

have agreed simply to pay them as necessary. The two issues of zero coupon municipals are present not for tax considerations but because they happened to be exceptional zeros at the time of purchase.

Obviously, for other types of investors other portfolio decisions would be more appropriate. A highly taxed investor would want a greater weighting of municipal zeros, for instance, or an investor more concerned with capital stability might invest only in the shortest zeros, trusting to self-discipline to reinvest for each additional year. Whatever the need or preference in a current income portfolio, serializing zeros of different maturities can provide it.

MUNICIPAL INVESTMENT TRUSTS

Another option you may want to consider for the income component of your portfolio is a municipal investment trust containing zeros and current income bonds.

A municipal trust permits you to receive federally untaxed current income as an indirect owner of a portfolio of municipal bonds. Most trusts give you the option of monthly, quarterly, semiannual, or annual payments. The trust matures as the municipal bonds in its portfolio mature, and your prorated portion of the trust's maturity value is returned to you as a repayment of principal.

Municipal investment trusts have only recently added a zero coupon bond component to their offerings. (The tax-exempt securities trust, remember, has a substantial component of zero municipals.) With the addition of municipal zeros to the trust, you receive federally untaxed capital growth along with federally untaxed current income.

Consequently, some municipal trusts are a combination of a current income fund and a tax-exempt securities trust, although there aren't any straight zero coupon municipal bond funds as yet on the market.

There are many municipal investment trusts on the market, and more are issued all the time, but not all contain a zero component. So you have to check the prospectus carefully if you want a fund with municipal zeros. One of the best-known municipal investment trusts is sponsored by Nuveen and Co., which pioneered the concept that's been adopted by other national financial intermediaries. The Kemper organization, which offers a family of mutual funds and other financial services, also issues municipal investment trusts. Gabriele, Hueglin & Cashman, Inc., a market maker in original issue zero coupon bonds, is an excellent source of municipal investment trusts, coupon-paying municipal bonds, and derivative zeros.

SUMMARY

As you've seen, zero coupon investments can be structured to provide current income, thus overcoming one criticism of zeros. Whether you're buying zeros that convert to current income investments or scheduling maturities to receive current income, you can take charge of your portfolio and use the convenience and predictability of zeros to receive the cash you need. With a clear and simple schedule, you can improvise the payments best for you, whether that means income from tax-deferred accounts, savings bonds, municipal zeros, or zero funds.

CHAPTER 10

ZERO COUPON INVESTMENTS AND THE CAPITAL GROWTH COMPONENT

By *capital growth* we generally mean investments that offer the chance for steady appreciation in price. Strictly speaking, zero coupon investments are not capital growth investments. However, zeros are serving functions which conventional growth investments used to serve. Many investors now prefer zeros over conventional growth investments, and others use them to supplement growth securities. You've already seen a few reasons why.

First, zeros provide predictable accumulations when held to maturity, and other growth investments provide no such guarantee of an ultimate payoff.

Second, zeros don't require intricate analysis, as do stocks, nor do they participate in limited markets, as do collectables, and they don't suffer the illiquidity and fees of real estate.

Third, throughout the 1980s, zeros have produced real and tax-adjusted returns that have exceeded historical returns from many types of growth investments.

Zeros certainly aren't going to push customary capital growth investments off the financial pages, because they don't provide the potentially unlimited price appreciation that other growth investments can offer. But, on the average, zero coupon securities deserve consideration in the capital growth component of the portfolio. Certainly, the first type of zero that has capital growth uses is the convertible corporate zero.

CONVERTIBLE CORPORATE ZEROS

Convertible corporate zeros offer the twin advantages of other convertible bonds: as bonds, they provide predictable payments upon maturity, and conversion privileges give the potential for capital gains from the underlying stock. Accordingly, these hybrid zeros can serve the growth component in the same way that other convertible corporate bonds do as a proxy for an equity investment.

However, you don't have to concentrate on zeros with special features in building the growth component of your investment plan. Derivative and original issue zeros as well as zero funds can also serve the growth element of the portfolio.

SHORT-TERM ZEROS IN PLACE OF OTHER GROWTH SECURITIES

Zeros maturing in five years provide steady gains while market price marches predictably toward par. As a near-term zero or short-term zero fund nears maturity, its price approaches par, in effect amortizing phantom interest. Even though this price increase isn't capital growth, short-term zeros will be worth more each year that you hold them, and steady increases are what you want in the capital growth component of the portfolio. Consequently, some investors, particularly in today's uncertain stock market and changing tax climate, prefer to invest for "growth" with short-term zeros.

They use short zeros because growth isn't steady with longer zeros, which are so sensitive to long-term interest rates. For instance, in 1989 let's say you bought a zero maturing in 20 years. In 1994, its price may not have appreciated substantially because the slightly decreased term of maturity — 15 years instead of 20 — won't overcome the influence of long-term interest rates. On the other hand, if you had initially bought a zero maturing in 1994, you would have seen some movement in price each year because the bond's five-year maturity would make it less vulnerable to long-term rates.

In addition, long-term zeros' sensitivity to interest rates may occasion sharp declines in prices, and that counteracts growth. Therefore, when using any zero coupon investment — corporates, municipals, derivatives, funds, CDs—as an alternative to standard growth investments, you should keep maturities short.

(Aggressive gains investors prefer the longest maturities, which provide true capital appreciation by coupling amortized phantom interest with declines in interest rates. This, however, is an aggressive gains strategy, not a long-term capital gains strategy, so we'll discuss it in the next chapter.)

In selecting zeros over standard growth investments, remember that you're usually expected to declare phantom interest yearly. Some advisors will insist that taxation on phantom interest should deter you entirely from holding zeros outside IRAs, Keoghs, and low-tax or tax-deferred accounts. You've already seen why such advice can be discounted.

USING ZEROS TO MEASURE GROWTH OPPORTUNITIES

By knowing that zeros will be worth a stated amount at the end of a given period, you can assess the desirability of a competing growth investment. A zero coupon investment offers a known return over a known period. If another growth investment doesn't offer the likelihood of equal performance during the same period, you know that it doesn't offer the above market returns that characterize a good capital growth investment, and your attention should be directed elsewhere. Thus, zeros are one standard for assessing the desirability of a conventional growth investment.

To illustrate, let's say that a real estate investment has the opportunity of producing at maximum a 30 percent total (not annualized) return in five years. However, over the same period, a high-quality zero may produce an equivalent return. What is the real growth opportunity offered by the real estate investment? In this case, it isn't much.

Every investment has an *opportunity cost*. In this case, the cost of undertaking another capital growth investment is forfeiting the known return of zeros. The zero will produce a known gain, whereas the *estimated maximum return* on the competing investment in this example is 30 percent. If any investment—real estate, stocks, gold, collectibles—can't produce the same return in a shorter period or a greater return in the same period, you're forfeiting the opportunity offered by the zero. The competing investment's opportunity cost is too high, and you can establish the opportunity cost for a given period by using zeros as your measurement.

USING ZEROS TO MINIMIZE CAPITAL LOSSES

The first principle of investing money is to not lose it, and that principle is served by the savings component with its assortment of zeros. The second principle is to invest in securities that provide known accumulations so you can estimate accurately how much you can make; that's the income component for which many types of zeros are also appropriate. The third principle is to select investments that may produce above average gains, and that's where the growth component is important.

The problem is that standard growth investments such as stocks don't guarantee you won't lose money, nor do they offer predictable returns over a known period. As a growth investor, you face an unavoidable tradeoff: you must trade the assurance of known gains for the uncertainty of greater possible gains and the possibility of losing money. But you can minimize the risk of capital loss by complementing stocks with zero coupon securities. In other words, you backstop your portfolio with zeros so that a fouled growth security doesn't ruin your total investment score

To see how you can make that happen, let's look at a portfolio of two securities, the first a growth stock and the second a zero coupon bond maturing in five years.

Your chosen stock is currently selling at $50. This stock is estimated to produce an average growth rate of 20 percent annually for five years. This estimate places the price for 100 shares—an investment of $5,000—at about $12,442 in five years. However, this return isn't assured.

Given that you're generally intending a holding period of five years, you look at Treasury zeros of 1994, currently selling for about $600 per $1,000 par. You can buy 10 Treasury zeros for $6,000 and secure an 8.5 percent return.

These zeros will be worth $10,000 in five years, an assured return. Consequently, of the $11,000 that you invested, only $1,000 is at risk of total loss. You have minimized the prospect of losing a major portion of your total investment.

Back Stopping Growth Stocks with Zero Coupon Bonds

	Worst Case Stock = 0% return	Intermediate Case Stock = 10% return	Best Case Stock = 20% return
Stock	$ 0	$ 8,053	$12,442
Zero	$10,000	$10,000	$10,000
Totals	$10,000	$18,053	$22,442

Here's the picture at the end of five years for the worst, intermediate, and best case scenarios. In this example, the highly unlikely worst case is defined as the stock being worth nothing at the end of five years. The intermediate case is defined as a 10 percent return. The best case means the stock does, in fact, produce its average expected return.

Even if the stock is worth zero at the end of five years, you're only out $1,000, disregarding commissions. If you'd invested the full $11,000 in the stock and the stock were worth nothing at the end of five years, you'd be out everything. Because a stock is virtually never worth zero, you have eliminated the possibility of an absolute loss and assured some gain by backstopping the stock component with a zero coupon component. This takes you a long way toward meeting the first principle of investing, namely, not to lose money.

If the stock produces its best anticipated gain in five years, your portfolio has produced $22,442. Obviously, if you had invested the full $11,000 in the stock, you would have earned more than $24,442. Unfortunately, you have no way of knowing that this will be the happy result. The more significant point is that you received $24,442 while eliminating all but $1,000 of absolute loss. Or, to look at it another way, you earned a 17.5 percent gain annually while reducing the risk of absolute loss of capital by combining the stock with zeros.

USING ZEROS TO MAXIMIZE PORTFOLIO RETURNS

The real merit of the backstopping strategy is apparent in the intermediate case where the stock produced only a 10 percent average annual return instead of the desired 20 percent.

If the stock performs at half its expected rate and is worth $8,053 over five years, your total portfolio value is $18,053 at the end of five years. That's about a 12.5 percent return from the two securities calculated on an annual basis. That's more than the percentage return from the zeros alone and more than the percentage return from the diminished performance of the stock.

You increased the total return of the portfolio even though the stock element performed less than expected. You have maximized your portfolio return in an environment of uncertainty while also minimizing your possibility of capital loss. And if the stock were to produce more than its 20 percent anticipated gain—say, 30 percent or 40 percent—you would really be in the gravy. You would have secured greater gains, limited the possibility of total loss, and achieved higher possibility of maximizing total return if the stock produced less than 20 percent.

If this scenario looks familiar, it should. This is essentially what the zero/stock funds do by mating a portfolio of common stocks and Treasury zeros. Note, also, that any of the zero coupon investments you've studied can be used in backstopping the capital growth component. Consequently, you have a host of alternatives in culling among zeros as companions to the capital growth component.

ZEROS AND THE GROWTH PORTFOLIO

The example we've just covered is that of a two-security portfolio—one stock, one bond. Your portfolio contains more than two securities and more than two types of investments. During most economic cycles and for most investors except the retired, however, growth securities constitute the majority of the portfolio. That fact makes it even more important for you to have zeros backstopping capital gains in your portfolio.

Growth investments are intended to produce measured, consistent, and optimal capital gains, and presumably they might frequently include some income securities like conventional bonds. The key words describing the midsection of growth are *measured, consistent,* and *optimal,* and those key words highlight the significance in accompanying zeros with growth securities.

How do you measure growth opportunities? You not only analyze an individual security, but you should also compare its possible returns against the certain accumulations offered by zeros.

How do you achieve consistent gains in the growth component? You not only trade a portfolio of attractive equities, but you should also invest in short-term zeros that produce steady accretions to maturity. Moreover, by backstopping capital growth investments with zeros, you also achieve assurance against absolute loss and relative predictability in uncertain markets for equities.

How do you attain optimal returns from the growth component? You not only select securities that produce their best-analysis gains, but you should also mate them with the predictable accumulations of zeros so that intermediate levels of gains are enhanced by the known compounding of zeros.

ZEROS AND BASE BUILDING

In the context of the growth portfolio, using zeros in this manner is called *base building*. Just as you can measure, stabilize, and maximize growth opportunities of a single stock with zeros, you can also use zeros to provide the consistency needed to evaluate and support a total growth portfolio.

Just how broad the percentage of zeros underpinning the total growth portfolio should be depends upon many factors. We've used the example of a 1:1 ratio because it illustrates the principle However, some investment situations might not call for such a more or less conservative ratio.

For instance, when the economy is in upswing and equities markets show greater potential, perhaps a ratio of 3:1 is more appropriate. That is, you might hold $3,000 in stocks for each $1,000 par value of zeros. In such a market and economic situation, growth stocks might not need the consistency of zeros behind them, and capital devoted to zeros is less productive than an investment in equities. On the other hand, when markets are stingy and equities unproductive, you might reverse the ratio. In such a market and economic climate unfavorable to stocks, the assurances of zeros commend a larger ratio to stocks.

Whatever the situation and your preferences, the concept is the same. By holding investment in growth vehicles to a proportion of the par value of zeros, you promote the purposes of growth and the principles of investing.

THE HOLDING PERIOD

Another topic to clarify is the notion of a holding period. In the example, we assumed an investor intended to hold a security for five years. Although that's a reasonable and typical estimate based on customary investor behavior, it's probably no longer the case that most investors intend to own equities as long as five years. Accordingly, if you intend to hold stocks for a fewer number of years, reduce the maturities of zeros in your base.

Some investors use their zero coupon savings—T-bills and money market funds—as the standard of maturities upon which they erect the growth component. Other investors find that standard to be too restrictive, so they select zeros of two or three years' maturity as the determinant of their base.

Some investors like to serialize maturities of zeros over several years and use them as the base for determining the proportion of capital devoted to growth. For instance, they have $20,000 in zeros maturing each year for eight years, and they allocate growth capital based upon funds coming due serially over several years. As a practical matter, you'll buy stocks with several different intended holding periods. It's equally practical to invest in zeros with maturities that match your varying holding periods.

SUMMARY

Whatever your choice of proportion or of maturities, investors striving for capital growth first ensure that there is a stable financial underpinning to their growth portfolio, and they create that stability with zero coupon securities. By so doing, they not only erect their investment plan upon a firm base, but they also maximize the use of zeros in other aspects of the capital growth component.

Even though zero coupon investments aren't typically associated with the capital growth component of the portfolio, they shouldn't be ignored there. Most of the zeros we've discussed can be useful in measuring the opportunity cost of standard growth vehicles, in substituting for those other vehicles, and in backstopping growth investments. And nearly all can be used to create the stable financial base that supports your portfolio of growth stocks. Undoubtedly, smart investment houses—and wise personal investors—will discover other ways in which zeros can be used in maximizing capital growth opportunities. For now, you need to move on to another aspect of the portfolio that zero coupon investments can serve—the aggressive gains component.

CHAPTER 11

ZERO COUPON INVESTMENTS AND THE AGGRESSIVE GAINS COMPONENT

In the preceding chapter you saw that zeros can be useful in the growth component of the portfolio, but we carefully pointed out that they don't, strictly speaking, produce capital gains. Now that we're looking at a different aspect of the portfolio—aggressive growth—we can recant that statement. When growth in their prices exceeds growth by approaching maturity, zeros do produce capital gains.

To illustrate, let's say that in 1986 you paid $400 for a corporate zero maturing in 2000. Ordinarily, this zero would amortize about $43 phantom interest each year, based on straight line amortization of phantom interest. Therefore, three years later in 1989 you'd expect this zero to be selling for about $528. However, when you pick up the financial pages to check your investment, perhaps this zero's current price is $700. The excess between price and amortized phantom interest is $100, and that difference *is* a capital gain.

Whenever a zero's market price exceeds its amortized phantom interest, you have a capital gain. That's true whether the zero is a corporate, derivative, or municipal issue. In a stable economy, market prices for zeros would never exceed their amortized phantom interest, and they would never produce a true capital gain. Fortunately—at least for aggressive zero investors—economywide interest rates are unstable. This market reality makes publicly traded zeros ideal for aggressive gains investors.

ZEROS FOR AGGRESSIVE GAINS

Aggressive gains are those which exceed market expectations, and the critical determinant of aggressive gains is volatility—sweeping upward and downward movements in price. Zeros are extremely sensitive to general interest rates because they pay interest only upon maturity. Without interim coupon payments to smooth out the interest rate trends, price is the sole determinant of yield, and price moves inversely to yield. Consequently, when the general course of interest rates falls. zeros appreciate sharply in price as their yields follow the general course of rates.

In order to have dramatic gains from an investment in zeros, you have to avoid zeros that don't fluctuate in price. That stricture takes EE Savings Bonds, zero CDs, most short-term zeros, and near-term zero funds out of the running as aggressive gains investments. The capital gains chapter highlighted short-term zeros for their lessened volatility. For aggressive gains, you shun short-term zeros and emphasize long-term zeros, which usually means a period of 15 to 20 years or more.

The aggressive investors' interest in the longest-running zeros is ironic because they don't intend to hold them anywhere near their term of maturity, nor are they interested in yield. The aggressive zero investor is interested solely in price appreciation, and the longer the term of maturity, the greater is the volatility that can produce dramatic capital gains.

Although they agree on the necessity of long-term securities, aggressive gains investors are divided about preferring municipal zeros or publicly listed Treasury and corporate zeros. Some investors point out that municipal zeros are disadvantaged in the aggressive gains component. They point out that publicly listed corporate and Treasury zeros have ready markets, whereas zero municipals have somewhat more limited markets. A ready market means not only that you can sell easily—absolutely essential for an aggressive strategy— but also that prices are printed in the daily financial pages, making it easier to decide when to sell.

ASPECTS OF AGGRESSIVE TRADING

Whatever your decision about the type of zero, you'll face several inescapable facts in trading zeros for aggressive purposes.

First, what goes up comes down, and the faster up, the faster down. Aggressive gains are possible with long-term zeros, but so are aggressive losses. With slight increases in general interest rates, prices of zeros plummet. (Price moves inversely to interest rates, remember.) Such is always the risk with aggressive investing.

Second, zeros generally produce a phantom interest tax liability while you hold them and when you sell them. Under post-1986 laws, the tax situation is simplified because interest and capital gains are taxed at the same rates. To some extent, this makes it attractive to trade taxable zeros held outside IRAs aggressively.

Third, commissions might be quite high as a percentage of investment and as a percentage of gain. Of course, if you buy and sell zeros through a sponsoring brokerage, you're subject to basis pricing, and that's usually less than an outright commission. But if you're trading zeros through listed exchanges, you'll pay a commission to buy and to sell. Generally, that commission will be one percent of face value purchased, although it can be higher. So if you buy $10,000 face value of long-term zeros, you'll pay around $200 for round-trip commissions. The same is true of selling. Commissions reduce your gains.

MANAGING ZEROS FOR AGGRESSIVE GAINS

If these considerations don't deter you, you might be interested in some techniques and wisdom from investors who've profited from the price fluctuations of long-term zeros.

First, most aggressive gains zero investors purchase only zeros backed by Treasury bonds. If they invest in long-term municipal zeros, they buy only the highest-rated issues. Aggressive zero investors are essentially interest rate speculators. Generally presumed to be free from default, government-backed zeros aren't influenced by profitability considerations that are accommodated by prices of corporate zeros. In other words, government-backed zeros are purer interest rate plays because interest rates are virtually the lone determinant of their price movements. Aggressive zero investors figure they'll have a hard enough time anticipating interest rate trends; they don't need the extra uncertainty associated with corporate zeros.

To a large extent, top-rated municipal zeros, especially those insured by backing agencies, are close substitutes for government-backed zeros. The municipal market, however, does not move lockstep in an absolute relationship with general interest rates and prices of government securities. They aren't "pure" interest rate plays to the extent that CATS, TIGRs, and other feline zeros are.

Second, aggressive zero investors usually aren't diversified. The cleanest aggressive zero strategy involves two investments: a money market fund and the longest-running, highest-quality zero available. When the investor expects interest rates to decline, he or she moves cash out of the money fund and into the chosen zero. When he or she feels the price run-up is over and interest rates are about to increase, the zeros are sold and the proceeds go back into the money fund, where it awaits the next cycle.

By holding their choice to one series of zeros, aggressive investors minimize commissions and simplify tracking their investment. If they held several series of zeros, they'd have to pay multiple commissions to buy and sell. Consolidating investments in one series of zeros also maximizes returns—if you're right about interest rates—whereas diversifying in several zeros to reduce risk will also reduce aggressive returns. The importance of consolidating an aggressive zero investment is another reason why aggressive investors prefer Treasury issues: no need to add default risk to market risk.

Third, aggressive but lesser capitalized zero coupon investors generally prefer zero funds over direct investment, although the low prices of long-term zeros do make them accessible to the average investor. The current zero funds are invested in felines, which accommodates the default factor, and they offer long-term choices in their portfolios, which is suitable for aggressive intentions. Fees or loads are usually less than commissions—although that may change—and the initial investment is small.

As you'll recall from Chapter 6, zero funds offer a selection of portfolios, long-term and short-term, within the fund. Generally investors who strive for aggressive gains through zero funds will rotate their capital between the longest-term portfolio in the fund and the shortest. That is, when they expect interest rates to fall, producing appreciation in the long-term portfolio, they phone the fund and direct their holdings into the long-term end of the fund. When they expect rates to fall, producing greater capital declines in long-term zeros, they phone the fund and switch back to the short end of the maturity spectrum, where volatility is less. Some issuers of zero funds also operate money market funds, the ultimate short-term zero fund. Aggressive investors move from the long-term portfolio to the money market fund by telephoning the issuer.

And while we're on the subject of aggressive gains and zero funds, don't forget the zero/commodity funds. These specialized funds don't offer the maneuverability of straight zero funds, nor are they interest rate plays, but the commodity side of the fund can produce exceptional gains while the zero side of the fund is assuring return of principal.

FOLLOWING INTEREST RATES

Obviously, aggressive zero investors are more than casually interested in the course of interest rates. No one is an infallible predictor of that economic variable, and most people aren't good at it when they try to be, but aggressive zero investors try harder than most. There are several indicators that they follow in their attempt to determine the direction of rates—the first being the maturities of investments in money market funds.

Money funds managers are professionals at following interest rates, and they arrange the investments in their funds to achieve the highest rates. When they expect interest rates to fall, they lengthen the maturities of investments under their control. Consequently, when you see that the average maturities of money market funds are lengthening (maturities are printed in *The Wall Street Journal* and in most financial pages weekly), you know the pros expect rates to fall. That's a clue to invest in long-term zeros, which appreciate with declines in rates.

Interest rate followers attempt to confirm professional managers' judgments by following the yields on conventional Treasury securities, which also are published in *The Wall Street Journal* and in most financial pages. When yields are falling—that is, when prices are increasing—that's confirmation that long-term zeros should be following suit.

In addition, there are other financial indicators of interest rates, and aggressive zero investors also track those. The federal funds rate—the interest rate that the Federal Reserve charges for short-term borrowings from member banks—indicates where the Federal Reserve would *like* to see general interest rates headed. When the Fed lowers the rate, that's considered an indication that the Fed wants to see general rates fall. The economy doesn't always reply in kind, but when it does, long-term zeros perform well.

Aggressive zero investors also pay attention to the rate of inflation. When it's falling, interest rates generally fall with it, and prices of zeros generally increase. A falling rate of inflation is usually a positive force for the prices of long-term zeros.

For a more thorough discussion of economic signals, interest rates, and investing during changing economies, pick up a copy of *Investing in Uncertain Times* by your author.

TRADING ZEROS ON MARGIN

Typically, the most aggressive bond investors have traded "on margin." Those who do put up a portion of the purchase price for bonds and borrow the rest from their brokerage. If interest rates decline sharply, these investors sell the bonds, repay the brokerage (with interest), and pocket their gains.

The Federal Reserve Bank establishes margin rules, and during the twentieth century the Fed has permitted investors to put up as little as 10 percent to purchase securities and has also shut down margin trading entirely. Individual brokerage firms may also impose restraints on margin trading. Subject to change, the following rules govern eligibility of trading zeros on margin.

- T-bills are marginable in all markets.
- CATS traded on public exchanges are marginable. Other Treasury zeros are maintained in markets by the sponsoring brokerages. They can be purchased on margin if the market-making brokerage will permit it.
- Zero coupon municipals are marginable as far as the Federal Reserve is concerned, but none of the major brokerage firms that your author contacted reported any experience with customers' buying municipal zeros on margin.
- The Federal Reserve has issued no opinion as to whether zero coupon corporate bonds are marginable. They presumably fall within the same margin criteria as other corporate bonds.

SUMMARY

So zero coupon investments do provide capital gains after all, and sometimes they provide them in a very short time. Long-term, publicly traded zeros can be excellent choices for the aggressive gains component of the portfolio, provided you have the temperament to weather their price fluctuations and the savvy to know when to get in and out of your investment. Whether you choose corporate, municipal, or Treasury zeros and zero funds, zeros can serve investors who want aggressive returns. Thus, you see that zeros can be of use in four of the five components of the portfolio. Now it's time to direct our attention to a component of the portfolio for which zeros are the undisputed investment of choice—the lump sum component.

CHAPTER 12

ZERO COUPON INVESTMENTS AND THE LUMP SUM COMPONENT

Even though zeros can be used to advantage in each of the portfolio components, they are perfect for the lump sum component, which is finally gaining the important investment recognition it deserves. The key to understanding its importance is in knowing the circumstances occasioning a single payment of capital.

The Uniform Gifts to Minors Account and the Individual Retirement Account are based upon need for lump sum accumulations, and the next three chapters are devoted to them. However, other circumstances served by the lump sum component include:

- The investor who will pay a balloon payment on a mortgage in a known number of years
- The investor who wants to accumulate capital for self-employment
- Investors who may need to support an aging parent, occasioning capital outlay for nursing home fees
- Divorced spouses whose decree makes one parent responsible for children's tuition at a distant date

Loyalty and experience don't outweigh the reality that older employees cost more than younger employees. Many of us feel that we'll be let go between age 55 and the time we can withdraw funds from an IRA or retirement plan. And many of us feel Social Security won't be there if we do reach retirement without interruptions in employment. These economic and emotional facts have generated concern for investments that provide predictable accumulations in the future.

CHARACTERISTICS OF THE LUMP SUM COMPONENT

The lump sum component is characterized by a known investment time period, or horizon, and by the need for a known quantity of funds, and we use *known* in an approximate and precise sense. You may, for example, *know* you'll need $50,000 *someday* to launch a business, or you may know you'll need $15,000 in 15 years to pay a mortgage balloon.

With fixed maturities and predictable accumulations, zeros are ideal for the lump sum component. Whether your investment horizon is weeks or decades, zero coupon vehicles (with one or two exceptions like EE Savings Bonds and variable rate corporates) give you a known par value on a fixed date for a known investment today. When you're looking for dependability in investment planning, zeros provide it, and dependability is what the lump sum component is all about.

APPROACHES TO THE LUMP SUM COMPONENT

First, let's take an investor with highly predictable circumstances, one who needs a known quantity of money in five years. Virtually any zero will accommodate this purpose—a corporate, municipal or derivative issue, a zero fund with a five-year portfolio, a zero CD— as long as the maturity coincides with the investor's purpose. All this investor does is calculate how much he or she will need and divide by $1,000, the par value of most zeros. If you need $10,000, buy 10 zeros, and so on.

Investors who don't know how much they'll need are in a different situation, because they don't know how much to invest now to meet that need. Take, for example, investors using the lump sum component as unemployment insurance. They estimate they need an uncertain sum to underpin their lives, but they don't know exactly how much or when. Investors in this circumstance follow one of two courses.

First, they may invest short-term, buying zeros maturing within five years or selecting near-term portfolios from zero funds. By keeping short, they maintain liquidity and minimize capital fluctuations. Should they be called upon to draw down their holdings, they're in a position to do so.

Second, these investors may estimate their period of vulnerability and set aside zeros that mature during the window of vulnerability. For instance, an investor might assume parents will need financial support in, say, 10 years. In this case, they'll select zeros maturing around this distant horizon and hold them for whatever eventuality presents itself.

When investors accommodate the lump sum component through a distant buy-and-hold strategy, they receive attractive yields for modest upfront investments. Zeros will fluctuate in price, but they're investing for maximum accumulations and accept volatility in prices. Whether they're direct purchasers of zeros or indirect investors, they invest for ultimate accumulations and stick with it.

These investors don't interpret *known investment horizon* literally. If they estimate they'll need funds in 10 years, that won't dissuade them from an attractive issue with a slightly longer or shorter maturity. If they need to reinvest matured zeros or to sell unmatured zeros, they can. So if you're concentrating the lump sum component on years after you're 55, for instance, you don't have to have every zero maturing when you're that age. Given that you're trying to deal with uncertainty in the first place, don't deny yourself flexibility.

We could continue with examples, but you get the idea. Investors who expect to need funds at particular times in the future pay attention to the lump sum component, and they rely upon zeros to provide the accumulations and dependability.

ZERO COUPON SECURITIES AND THE LUMP SUM COMPONENT

T-bills are of merit to investors who like to keep their zeros short. Also, near-term zeros and short-term zero funds are acceptable for their market-level returns and minimal capital fluctuation.

Zero coupon CDs present some problems, as do EE Savings Bonds, for some lump sum strategies. These zeros are illiquid. Consequently, they're used by investors as an adjunct to other elements of the lump sum component.

Zero funds can be useful, particularly for investors who don't have lots of initial capital or who prefer to contribute over time to the lump sum component. By starting with $1,000 and contributing fixed or variable amounts over time, you can build a sizable lump sum component without large initial investment.

Corporate and Treasury zeros are ideal. Available in a range of maturities and safe against default, they're liquid in public or broker-maintained markets and provide the necessary predictability. They do, however, usually generate a current federal tax liability when held outside tax-deferred accounts. Many investors regard that as an advantage, or at least as the price they pay for serving other portfolio intentions.

Given what the lump sum component is intended to do, however, most investors prefer high-quality zero coupon municipals, even if they're in minimal tax brackets. They reason that their incomes and tax burdens will grow. Therefore, when investing long-term they anticipate the need for accumulations from both a tax view and an investment view.

(Taxes are one reason why some investors elect not to defer taxation of EE Savings Bonds. If you're in the 15 percent bracket now and expect to progress to higher brackets, you might be better off paying the IRS as you go rather than wait until EEs mature and pay tax when your liability is greater.)

Because of unpredictable maturity values, municipal investment trusts don't work optimally in the lump sum component. They're moderately useful, but they don't provide known accumulations that are a comfort in the lump sum component. Tax-exempt securities trusts are a similar situation. Although they have an advantage as indirect investments in municipal zeros, they, too, have only an approximate maturity.

Convertible municipals shouldn't be overlooked. They provide the same accumulations as do zero municipals, and their conversion to coupon-paying bonds just might provide income you need without selling the bond.

The great thing about the growing variety of zero coupon investments is that you can apportion the lump sum component among them. If you can't find a Treasury zero maturing when you need it, look into zero funds or another alternative. You can mix and match differing types of zeros, managing taxes, maturities, and quality to advantage. And if the market isn't presenting sterling opportunities during your lump sum horizon, invest in T-bills, money funds, or short-term zero fund portfolios until the prices, rates, and maturities of other zeros attract your attention.

BLENDING THE LUMP SUM COMPONENT

In addition to mixing and matching for your own portfolio, husbands and wives—even business partners—blend zeros for synergy in the lump sum component. Considerations of tax status, age, life expectations, and career objectives can be accommodated among investors who are partners in any sense.

Take the case of a husband who is older than his wife. In this case, the wife might invest in her zeros and the husband in his zeros rather than own them jointly. If the husband dies first, inheritance considerations might make this an advantaged strategy. As always, consult tax counsel when apportioning investments.

Also, the husband and wife will blend zeros to accommodate their life together. If the wife is investing for a fixed horizon, the husband might concentrate his investment horizon with regard to her selection of maturities.

Or take the case of business partners. There may be a time when one partner will buy the other's interest in the business. An investment in zeros can accumulate funds for that purpose. If the partnership is congenial and partners understand the plan, the selling partner can arrange his lump sum investments knowing that the buying partner is, in effect, contributing to the seller's lump sum component.

Many permutations are possible. Children can arrange lump sum investments in consideration of their parents' selection of maturities. Parents can plan in consideration of their children's portfolios of zeros. To borrow from the sociologist's terminology, you can have a nuclear family of zeros.

One couple for whom your author is an investment advisor has been doing precisely that for several years. Both spouses are in their late 30s, and they've been arranging a portfolio of zeros following a lump sum strategy to meet four anticipated needs: providing a

Zero Coupon Maturity Dates and Par Values	
Year of Maturity	Par Values
1990 (Age 42)	
1991	
1992	
1993	$ 15,000
1994	$ 15,000
1995	$ 15,000 Child's Tuition
1996	$ 15,000
1997	
1998 (Age 50)	$ 25,000 — Mortgage Balloon Payment
1999	
2000	
2001	
2002	
2003 (Age 55)	$ 50,000 — Unemployment Fund
2004	
2005	
2006	
2007	
2008	
2009	
2010	
2011	
2012	
2013 (Age 65)	$100,000 IRA Maturities
	$100,000

base level of tuition support for their child, anticipating a mortgage balloon payment, setting aside a sum as unemployment insurance, and starting a retirement plan.

The foregoing is an actual page out of the couple's planning for a lump sum component. Their plan is to have the required quantity of zeros maturing for each year indicated. In some cases they've not yet reached their goals, but by calling upon their knowledge of the lump sum component and the appropriateness of zeros, they can meet their goals. All zeros held outside tax-deferred plans are municipals, and those in their IRAs are Treasury zeros. They intend to fill in the missing maturities as they age and as financial markets provide attractive issues. If hardship demands that they cash their zeros before maturity, they'll have capital available. If their program proceeds uninterrupted, their goals will be secured in a few years.

SUMMARY

For many reasons, the lump sum component of the portfolio has been receiving increased attention from wise investors and investment advisors. There are many occasions in life that call for a sizable outlay of capital, and zero coupon investments can help to anticipate them. By mixing and matching zeros, investors who look ahead can maximize their advantages and opportunities.

With this discussion, we end our examination of how zeros can serve each of the five portfolio elements. You still have two more chapters that deal with selected accounts in service to the lump sum component, the UGMA and the IRA, so let's move on to those.

CHAPTER 13

USING ZEROS
FOR TUITION
PLANNING

Next to retirement, investing to meet tuition expenses is among the foremost concerns of American parents. There's little wonder that this is so, as some authorities estimate rearing one child to age 18 will require one third of your net income—and that's before college expenses kick in at 18.

The customary problem with tuition planning is that most parents, unavoidably or not, start too late. It's tough to meet four years of college education by starting two years before sons and daughters start college unless your income has increased substantially On the other hand, it's not impossible.

The second customary problem is that parents will hold securities earmarked for tuition in their own names. You may have it in mind that the investment belongs to your child, but the tax authorities won't see it that way. They'll expect securities held in your name to be taxed at your personal rates, and taxes reduce investment returns.

Finally, parents don't realize that tuition planning is a fixed sum, fixed time investment problem—in short, a circumstance more suited for the lump sum component of the portfolio than for the growth component. You're going to need a relatively predictable amount at a predictable time, and as that time approaches, you can less tolerate capital losses associated with capital growth. All of these circumstances make zero coupon bonds ideal for tuition planning.

UNIFORM GIFTS TO MINORS ACCOUNTS (UGMA)

Assuming you're not in the position of establishing elaborate legal trusts, the favored way to accommodate children's tuition expenses is by opening Uniform Gifts to Minors Accounts.

The UGMA is a specialized account to which parents or related parties contribute cash or investments. Established with a bank, broker, or mutual fund, the account belongs to the child, as do the securities you purchase or contribute to the account. Each parent can contribute up to $10,000 yearly to each child without incurring gift taxes. One parent is usually the custodian for the account, although some states require a trustee to fulfill this obligation. The custodian directs investments in the account, and the proceeds revert to the child when he or she attains majority.

Two advantages commend the UGMA. First, its assets are separate from your assets. Should estate taxes become a consideration, the UGMA is not part of your estate and therefore is separate from estate proceedings. Second, a portion of investment returns in the UGMA will escape taxation.

Tax merits of UGMAs now are not as broad as before the Internal Revenue Code of 1986. Under present law, the first $500 of investment returns in the account escapes taxation because that sum is offset by the child's personal income tax exclusion. The $500 of investment income that otherwise would be fully taxed is untaxed.

The next tier of $500 in investment income in the UGMA is taxed at the child's personal rate—15% in most cases under 1988 law. However, investment returns above $1,000 are taxed at parents' personal tax rates, not the child's, as under previous law, until the child reaches age 14. At age 14, the child pays income tax at his or her personal tax rate on all investment returns in the UGMA.

CORPORATE AND TREASURY ZEROS
IN THE UGMA

Otherwise fully taxable, investment grade corporate and Treasury zeros are especially advantaged if their phantom yearly interest accrues to less than $500 in UGMAs for preadolescent children. If managed with regard for the compound taxable interest formula in

Chapter One, their phantom interest won't be taxed. Being untaxed, their tax equivalent yield will be even higher.

As you've seen, corporate zeros typically cost less and yield more than comparable Treasury zeros while providing the same advantages of a known maturity value. For this reason, combined with the $500 untaxed yearly accumulation now possible in UGMAs, you can buy corporate zeros for your child and enjoy the higher yield untaxed.

Although costing a bit more and yielding a bit less than corporates, Treasury zeros offer the same happy tax and investment circumstances for your younger children, and they are protected against default.

The problem for children under age 14, if it becomes a problem, occurs when phantom yearly interest on corporate and Treasury zeros exceeds $500. Beyond that threshold, the next $500 of interest is taxed at the child's rate, and any amount above that is taxed at your personal rates, and taxes offset the advantages of the UGMA. You have two alternatives in managing this situation.

First, you can concentrate fully taxable zeros in short maturities and reinvest par value of the bonds when they mature. You buy that quantity of short-term bonds that will not exceed $500 in yearly phantom interest, take advantage of the UGMA tax break, and position your child for later investment that preserves yield and tax features.

Second, you can buy fully taxable zeros of longer maturity as the floor of a continuing portfolio, a particularly advantaged strategy if you start the UGMA early. In this case, you select zeros that will produce less than $500 of phantom yearly interest for a longer period, say, until your child is 14. You'll enjoy the sustained, untaxed compounding for a longer period.

If you're willing, you can buy enough zeros to produce $1,000 in taxable phantom interest in the UGMA, taking your smaller tax lumps on that second $500 taxable to the child, but postponing income taxable at your rates.

Also, the key tax phrase is *all returns* in the UGMA, including capital growth. If you buy long-term zeros that appreciate in price beyond compound accreted value to date, you can sell to preserve the capital gain and reinvest in shorter zeros or other types of bonds.

Fully taxable zeros can work for adolescents 14 and older, because all phantom taxable interest will be taxed at their rates, not your presumably higher income tax rates. At that tax point, however, you'll probably want municipal zeros.

MUNICIPAL ZEROS FOR UGMAs

In many respects, the post-1986 tax code invites you to shuck the whole tax problem through purchasing municipal zeros in the UGMA. Formerly a poor idea, today it makes more sense to buy municipal zeros for children. For one thing, you avoid the federal tax consequences of all interest payments in the UGMA. There's no need to struggle over the compound tax and interest formula to determine when taxable zeros will penetrate the $500 or $1,000 threshold, because municipal zeros aren't federally taxed. For another consideration, municipal zeros are now sufficiently abundant in number that you don't have to hunt them down. They offer the same dependability of accumulations that all zeros do and are ideal for a lump sum portfolio like the UGMA. Review Chapter Three for the advantages of municipal zeros.

Populating the UGMA with municipal zeros is especially wise if you anticipate an increase in federal tax rates, and most investors do expect that to happen. If personal tax rates increase, returns in your child's UGMA will be affected. On a tax equivalent basis, any untaxed returns in the UGMA will be greater, including fully taxable bonds that escape taxation, but so will the federally untaxed returns of municipal zeros

SAVINGS BONDS

In place of or in addition to the UGMA, you can buy EE Savings Bonds for your children. Name the child as sole owner at the time the bond is purchased, and no further paperwork is required for accreted interest to be taxable at the child's rate.

The original zero coupon investment is limited in that it offers only 12-year maturities, and its sliding scale of interest produces meager returns in the early years. Accordingly, the EE bond is not as versatile as other zeros, but it grants other advantages.

Tax on accreted interest can be declared yearly or deferred until paid at maturity or upon being cashed in, so you can attend to the tax consequences that prevail under the new laws. Interest also is exempt from state and local taxation. However, one problem you face in deferring tax on EE bond interest is that Congress may have raised personal tax rates by the time the bond matures and tax on accreted interest becomes payable. Higher tax brackets cut into the child's accumulations.

Held longer than five years, an EE bond pays 85 percent of the rate on five-year Treasuries, adjusted every six months. Interest accrual will increase as rates on five-year Treasury notes increase—and advantage as interest rates increase—but will never accrue at less than the base rate of 6 percent if interest rates fall. You receive interest rate and market risk protection because EE bonds will never be worth less than purchase price.

SERIALIZED ZEROS IN THE UGMA

If you opt for zeros, the easiest strategy to follow is to buy zeros maturing during the years of your child's college education, anticipating how much you'll need for freshman year, sophomore, and so on. You stage zeros to mature over a span of four or however many college years, and you allocate your zeros accordingly. When the zeros mature, the money is there for college.

In general, financial advisors suggest that you'll want at least $10,000 as a base level of accumulations for each college year of each child. Obviously, $10,000 may not be enough when your children are ready for college, but $10,000 is a base level for planning. Below is a representative UGMA portfolio based on prices of Treasury zeros available in 1988. Let's assume that a child will start college in 2000 and remain through 2003.

An investment of $12,713 serialized in these Treasury zeros will produce $40,000 in $10,000 increments between 2000 and 2003. These four issues of zeros will produce approximately $852.45 in phantom interest during the first year Therefore, you'll have to de-

Year	Yield to Maturity	Price per $10,000	Maturity Value
2000	8.83%	$ 3,674	$10,000
2001	8.85%	$ 3,356	$10,000
2002	8.91%	$ 2,988	$10,000
2003	8.87%	$ 2,695	$10,000
Totals		$12,713	$40,000

clare $352.45 in taxable phantom interest. Taxed at the child's rate of presumably 15%, that's a $52.87 tax bill the first year. The tax bill will, of course, increase as the zeros compound toward maturity. If you invest in federally untaxed municipals, you avoid the federal tax problem.

Should you be financially fortunate, you can buy a sufficient quantity of zeros at one time, or you can patch the UGMA together piecemeal, buying a few thousand dollars face value this year, next year, and so on. In either case, you'll be able to assemble a base level of accumulations for college expenses during the years indicated.

CONTINUING INVESTMENT

Many parents can't afford to settle the child's future tuition needs at one time, although many more parents could be in such a fortunate position if they knew more about the low prices on zeros of distant maturities. If you intend to make continuing, small investments in a UGMA over a period of years, consider a bond fund.

Corporate, Treasury, and municipal funds permit low initial investments and lower subsequent investments as you embark on the road to paying for tuition. They contain the bonds you'd normally select for the UGMA, and they permit you to accumulate shares as you can afford them. The fund also will maintain all your records, a welcome function at year-end tax time.

Zero coupon bond funds can be particularly useful for the piece-meal investor. Maturing in set years—perhaps years that coincide with your child's college years—zero funds let you buy zeros a little bit at a time and still preserve the advantages of directly purchased zeros. You'll want all returns reinvested in additional shares of the fund for maximum accumulations. A further consideration is that you can use switch privileges to move among bond funds, particularly from a corporate or Treasury fund into a municipal fund as taxes become a consideration.

Don't forget TBRs. Their smaller par values mean smaller initial investment. You'll be able to set aside something for your children in a zero that offers all the attractions of more conventional derivative zeros.

TOO LITTLE TOO LATE

If you wake up one morning and discover that your baby is suddenly three years from freshmanhood, there's not a lot you can do to prepare unless you have a substantial capital wad at your disposal. Lacking it, you still have some options.

First, remember that you have four years of college to prepare for, and that fourth year is seven years away. Zero coupon bonds maturing in seven years will carry some fair prices and yields. You can take care of the more distant college years first, and that's better than throwing up your hands in resignation.

Second, consider bonds maturing beyond the years your child will be in college, say, ten years rather than seven as in this example.

A longer zero will carry a more advantaged price, and that price will stabilize near par as the zeros mature. You can sell the zero before maturity to pay some part of college tuition, taking advantage of its lower initial cost. Further, if interest rates fall, your zero will appreciate. Capital appreciation might add an extra increment to your tuition funds.

In addition, longer bonds typically offer a higher coupon or current yield than shorter bonds. You can increase tuition funds, at least slightly, with yields from longer bonds. Prices might also increase, providing another source of income.

Review your personal portfolio holdings to see what can be maneuvered into zeros for your child's education. This is an excellent idea on a continuing basis, but it's necessary if you're scrambling to meet tuition. If you're holding an unproductive stock, a noncompetitive bond, or any financial asset that isn't performing, convert it to the tuition portfolio.

Check the tax status of your investments. Examine corporate bonds in particular, because their interest is fully taxed. As a general rule, most investors can substitute Treasuries for corporates and save on taxes, as Treasuries aren't municipally taxable. Don't forget double-dipper municipal bonds for exemption from federal and state tax. The money you save on taxes or the extra income you can find will add to the tuition account.

All these are interim measures for the tardy planner, but they're also part of the battery of tricks that a conversant zero coupon investor knows how to employ when the situation demands them.

SUMMARY

A college education is part of the American dream that parents hold for their children, and paying for it doesn't have to be a nightmare. By starting early, holding assets in UGMAs, and relying upon the features of zero coupon securities, parents can achieve a base level of tuition support for children with minimal distortion to their own portfolios.

The most straightforward strategy is to regard the UGMA as a problem for the lump sum component of the portfolio. Purchase zero coupon bonds, especially municipals under the new tax laws, maturing during the years of your child's education and earmark their maturity value for tuition. Again, federally untaxed municipals can avoid the problems presented by fully taxable bonds in the UGMA.

Zero funds are your best choice for long-term accumulations through small, regular investments. The choice of funds, switch privileges, and recordkeeping services commend funds for many tuition-minded investors.

CHAPTER 14

ZERO COUPON INVESTMENTS AND RETIREMENT ACCOUNTS

It should be obvious why zero coupon investments have become the most popular investments for Individual Retirement Accounts and Self-Employed Retirement Plans (SERPs, formerly called Keogh Plans). Their highly predictable returns enable you to know exactly how much your IRA or SERP will be worth when your zeros mature, and predictability is a great advantage in retirement planning.

Their range of maturities fits your retirement plan whether you're retiring this year or a quarter of a century from now. Low prices for distant maturities permit younger investors with lower salaries to have long-term growth with modest investments. With zeros' handsome accumulations, you can earn 10 times your investment in 20 to 25 years, and you can triple or quadruple your money in 8 to 12 years.

Zeros also maximize tax-deferral advantages of IRAs and SERPs, as their phantom income isn't taxable until you receive it from your plan. Zeros are easy to buy. Every major brokerage sells its own zeros, and CATS are traded on public exchanges at reduced commissions from discount brokers. With the astonishing number of zero investments available, you can choose zero CDs, corporate zeros, and zero bond funds if you can't find derivative zeros to meet your needs.

Whatever your preference for types of zeros in your IRA or SERP, you'll get the most from them if you know how to manage them. There's no formula for making the most of zeros, but you'll want to consider quality and maturity first when you're selecting zeros for IRAs and SERPs.

MANAGING QUALITY

Derivatives are the highest quality zeros due to their underpinning by Treasury bonds, and zero funds holding derivative zeros are a close second. Therefore, if you're looking for the highest quality, stick with U.S. government-backed issues.

Zero coupon CDs backed by FDIC or FSLIC insurance are close to derivatives in quality, but there's no substitute for backing by Treasury bonds. Corporate zeros can be suitable for IRAs, but when investing long term, the quality differential with derivatives is probably worth choosing them over corporates.

There are few absolutes in the world of investing, but one of them is that zeros of less than investment grade do not belong in your tax-deferred portfolio. In fact, many investors refuse corporate zeros of less than a AA rating. There are at least two reasons for this cautiousness.

First, your retirement portfolio demands the highest assurances against default. This is true generally, as a retirement account is no place to be losing money. More specifically, a retirement portfolio permits you the advantage of long-term holdings for maximum compounding, and the security of long-term holdings is enhanced by top quality against default.

Second, the yield differential of lesser quality zeros is rarely sufficient to offset their lesser assurances against default. In late 1988, for example, Treasury derivative zeros were offering consistent 8.5% to 9% yields to maturity while lower-end investment grade corporate zeros offered slightly above 9%. At the same time, clearly speculative corporate zeros were offering 12% yields.

These latter zeros simply have no place in a quality portfolio; the former weren't offering an adequate inducement to prefer them over Treasuries. This pattern of late 1988 was by no means unique. During much of the time that publicly traded zero coupon securities have been available, the yield differential has not compensated for the quality differential.

MANAGING MATURITIES—THE CLIFF STRATEGY

In picking zeros of a specific maturity, your first option is the buy-and-hold strategy: select issues maturing during your expected years of retirement and hold them. This is the easiest strategy if you don't want to monitor zeros closely, but it requires you to select highest quality zeros.

There are two subsets of the buy-and-hold strategy for zeros in IRAs and SERPs. First, you can time all your zeros to mature during the year in which you expect to retire. The *cliff strategy*, as it's known, has two advantages: you have all your zeros in one place, making it easier to maneuver them if you want to sell prior to maturity, and when the zeros mature all at the same time, presumably the year you retire, you can reapportion the proceeds as retirement needs and market conditions dictate.

As Figure 14–1 indicates, an investor expects to retire in 2015. His or her cliff strategy, therefore, is to buy, over many years between now and then, Treasury or corporate zeros maturing in 2015. Upon retirement, the investor will convert the accumulated value of the zeros into current income investments—choices might include conventional bonds or high dividend stocks—that provide semiannual or quarterly income to supplement pensions and Social Security. (For a more thorough discussion of those income investments and their uses, pick up a copy of *The Income Investor—Choosing Investments That Pay Cash Today and Tomorrow,* also written by your author.)

FIGURE 14–1
Zeros for Retirement Planning Buy-and-Hold Intentions Cliff Strategy

Year	Accumulations
2012	
2013	
2014	
2015	$100,000*
2016	
2017	
2018	
2019	

*Maturity value to be reapportioned in 2015 for continuing income

As of late 1988, Treasury zeros maturing in 2015 cost $100 and offer 8.8 percent to maturity. Accordingly, the investor putting $2,000 into an IRA could have purchased $20,000 worth of zeros maturing in 2015. This investor is many years from retirement, so he or she will have decades in which to continue taking advantage of these low prices.

However, there is a potential disadvantage to this strategy. If you stack your IRA with zeros maturing in the same year, prices will rise and yields will fall as you buy the same zeros closer to maturity. That is, if you buy zeros today maturing in 2015, you'll pay $100 and receive $1,000. If you buy those same zeros in the year 2000, for instance, they will cost more and yield less. This is the price, figuratively and literally, that you'll pay for the convenience of consolidation and maneuverability in the year you retire.

MANAGING MATURITIES—THE INCOME STREAM ARRANGEMENT

The second subset of the buy-and-hold strategy offers you a way around the disadvantage of the cliff strategy. It is called an *income stream arrangement.* In following an income stream arrangement, you pick zeros maturing during the successive years of your retirement. One series of zeros matures when you're 65, another when you're 66, and so on through your estimated life expectancy. The strategy is so named because maturing zeros provide you with a stream of income each year during retirement.

Figure 14–2 illustrates how an investor can ladder zeros to produce a continuing stream of income during each year of his or her retirement. Instead of cliffing all zeros to mature in 2015 and then reapportioning the income at retirement, the investor creates a future income stream as a continuing strategy for IRA investment. This year, he or she invests, for example, $2,000 in zeros maturing in 2015. The following year, the investor buys zeros maturing in 2016, and so on for each additional year to which contributions are made to the IRA.

If the income stream strategy looks familiar, it should. In Chapter 8 we took a single sum of money and spread it out among zeros of serialized maturity. Here we take the $2,000 maximum *yearly*

FIGURE 14-2
Zeros for Retirement Planning Buy-and-Hold Intentions Income Stream Strategy

Year	Accumulations
2012	
2013	
2014	
2015	$20,000
2016	$20,000
2017	$20,000
2018	$20,000
2019	$20,000

IRA contribution and serialize deposits each year for many years to produce current income during retirement.

This strategy also has several advantages. It lets you fill in your IRA at advantaged prices and yields, and the income stream strategy allows you to benefit from new zeros that come on the market in the future. At early 1989, the longest Treasury zeros had about 30-year maturities. Someone who is, say, 35 years from retirement could buy the 30-year zeros and wait for zeros of more distant maturities to be offered. He or she could then add those to the IRA and wait for even more distant maturities to become available.

Finally, the income stream strategy offers the greatest predictability and ease of management. In buying zeros, you know how much they'll be worth when they mature, and you merely cash the proceeds each year of your retirement.

MANAGING ZEROS ACCORDING TO INTEREST RATES

However, the buy-and-hold strategy isn't the only alternative, nor are quality and maturity the only considerations in managing zeros. Some investors prefer to manage their IRAs and SERPs more actively than the buy-and-hold strategy permits, so they pay greatest attention to another characteristic of zeros, namely, interest rates.

When it comes to managing zeros through interest rates, you have two choices. You can choose the highest rate for the shortest time or the highest rate for the longest time. Let's look at three Treasury issues and examine how you might evaluate them in managing your zeros. Prices and interest rates presented here are several years old. We deliberately chose that time period because former levels of interest rates, as opposed to the rates of early 1989, better illustrate your range of choices, and with the benefit of hindsight, you can more easily see the result of choices.

We've assumed an investment of $2,000, meaning you could have bought 3, 12, or 26 zeros, respectively, for total accumulations of $3,000, $12,000, or $26,000 at the time these prices and yields were in effect.

You might have wanted to invest in the highest yield for the shortest time. You would have purchased the 1989 CATS, then priced at $630 to yield 11.6 percent.

As a yield-conscious investor, you would have argued that the shorter maturity presented a high interest rate and greater reinvestment opportunity. At that time, you could have surmised that rates would be higher in 1989 when these zeros mature. Therefore, you could have accepted the 11.6 percent offered by the CATS of 1989, held the issue to maturity, and planned to reexamine investment opportunities in 1989. As it turned out, you would have been wrong, but your thinking was reasonable, for most investors prefer shorter maturities when yields are undifferentiated, as is the case here where yields were within .4 percent of each other.

However, as a yield-conscious investor, your strategy might have been to lock in the highest rate for the longest period. In this case, you would have chosen the CATS of 2001, then priced at $150 per $1,000 par for a yield of 12 percent and a total accumulation of $12,000.

There was certainly reason for preferring the 12 percent offered by the CATS of 2001. The course of interest rates is erratic. After all, the CATS of 2008 were yielding the same as the CATS of 1989. You might have reasoned that yields could increase in the future, but

Maturity	Price	Yield to Maturity	Par Value
May 1989	$630	11.6%	$ 3,000
Aug 2001	150	12.0%	$12,000
Aug 2008	72	11.6%	$26,000

you also would have known they might decline, as in fact they did. Therefore, why not take the highest rate for the longest time? This, too, was reasonable thinking and an acceptable investment strategy that turned out to be right for the economy that has emerged today.

Accordingly, as a yield-conscious investor, you could have been "right" whether you selected an interest rate of 11.6 or 12 percent, for sound reasoning backed your thinking. However, you'll notice that you had a third option—the CATS of 2008.

MANAGING TOTAL ACCUMULATIONS

The yield-conscious investor would have thought it foolish to prefer the securities maturing in 2008. Their yield of 11.6 percent was the same as the CATS of 1989 and less than the 12 percent on the CATS of 2001. This zero offered neither maximum interest nor opportunity to reinvest advantageously if rates rose. What could have been its attraction?

The answer is that some IRA/SERP investors prefer to invest for maximum total accumulations regardless of yield.

With the CATS of 2008 as your choice, a $2,000 investment would have increased more than tenfold. But there were two additional advantages to this issue of zeros. It was the most predictable among all the zeros, for investors selecting briefer maturities risk receiving lower rates when they roll over matured zeros, as in fact happened. In addition, investing long term minimizes commissions.

Minimizing commissions is important because zeros generate no current income to counterbalance commissions. Commissions for zeros detract from capital because they can't be paid from coupon interest. Commissions are also important for another reason—compounding.

With the CATS of 2008 selling at $72, every $72 you pay in commissions then denies you $1,000 in 2008. The more often your CATS mature, the more often you must reinvest; the more often you must reinvest, the more often you must pay commissions; the more commissions you pay, the greater the compounding you lose for not selecting the longer maturity. Consequently, you may end up with more retirement cash even though you receive less in interest by selecting the longest maturity. Therefore, from the point of view of total accumulations, including foregone commissions, you would prefer the CATS of 2008.

(As we've noted, you minimize commissions on zeros by purchasing from the underwriting brokerage when they're initially issued or by purchasing them, also without commission, from the inventory of the underwriting brokerage after they're initially offered.)

MANAGING FOR AGGRESSIVE GAINS

If you'll be retiring in a few years, you might not see much attraction in zeros maturing in 20 years or longer. If so, reconsider, because long-term zeros present another strategy for managing your IRA and SERP: investing for aggressive capital gains.

As we've noted so often, zeros are exceptionally volatile because their return is paid at maturity. Consequently, their prices fluctuate dramatically, and the longer the term to maturity, the greater the fluctuations. To take advantage of hindsight and the previous example, CATS maturing in 2008, priced at $72 in 1986, are today priced at $182. An aggressive IRA or SERP investor could have doubled his money even though these zeros are still decades from maturity.

Aggressive management of zeros isn't appropriate for everyone, and given the extraordinary gains possible with limited trading, aggressive trading might prove most rewarding only to your stockbroker. But more confident and sophisticated investors can certainly consider the possibilities of long-term zeros as short-term holdings.

TAKING ADVANTAGE OF AGGRESSIVE GAINS

There is another point to be made about taking gains from the aggressive appreciation that zeros produce when economywide interest rates fall. You might want to sell your appreciated zeros to preserve your gains by shortening their maturities. The CATS of 2008 are an excellent illustration.

Priced today at $182, they produce an 8.8 percent yield to maturity in 2008. However, today you can secure an 8.5 percent yield to maturity on zeros priced at $600 and maturing in 1994. Accordingly, you can sell the 26 zeros of 2008 at today's current market price and reinvest the $4,732 in seven zeros of 1994 to secure essentially the same yield—although, of course, only $7,000 in par value. this maneuver permits you to seal in the zeros' capital appreciation and to await subsequent opportunities when the newly purchased, shorter zeros mature in 1994.

You might not have been initially interested in aggressive gains from zeros, but changes in economywide rates produced them, and you can take advantage by shortening maturities.

ZERO COUPON FUNDS FOR IRAS AND KEOGHS

Zero bond funds offer an excellent opportunity to manage a portfolio or zeros with discipline, simplicity, and profit. Zero funds investing in derivatives are approved for IRAs and SERPs, and you can select the portfolio or portfolios within the fund that meet your objectives. Zero funds also permit modest initial and subsequent investments, letting you set aside what you can if you can't make the full $2,000 permitted yearly for your IRA.

Over long periods, dollar-cost averaging can work powerfully for IRA contributions to zero funds. You can have the growth of zeros plus the purchase advantages associated with dollar-costing. This in itself may make zero funds your most advantageous choice for an IRA or SERP.

CORPORATE AND CONVERTIBLE ZEROS

Corporate zeros are acceptable for IRAs and SERPs, although it's usually wise not to let them constitute a formidable percentage of your holdings. Profitability of the issuer is a major consideration when buying corporate zeros, especially with long-term zeros. Derivatives avoid profitability considerations because they're virtually immune to default, and, as of late 1988, derivatives offered a greater range of maturities than corporate zeros currently offer. These two considerations generally dictate a preference for derivatives over corporates.

However, it may be that a particular investment-grade corporate zero offers a maturity that fits your needs. If so, there's certainly nothing wrong in mixing corporate zeros with your derivatives, CDs, and zero funds as part of your IRA or SERP.

Convertible corporate zeros also can have a place in your IRA. Their conversion features offer the chance for gains from the underlying common or preferred stock, and as zero coupon bonds they provide the predictable capital accumulations that are favored for IRAs. Given that corporate convertible zeros are so few in number at present, however, you might be better off salting your IRA with conventional coupon-paying convertible corporate debentures if your strategy is to select corporate debentures as equity-equivalent investments. Conventional convertible corporate debentures are greater in number and give you better variety and potential for profitability.

ZERO COUPON CERTIFICATES OF DEPOSIT

Zero CDs can be useful for IRAs and SERPs, but limited maturities generally dictate that they be used to fill in missing or unattractive maturity dates elsewhere in the portfolio of zeros. The chief drawback to having zero CDs as your main IRA investment is what's called an *overlapping plate problem.*

To illustrate, let's say that this year you buy a zero CD maturing in 10 years. Next year you do the same, and likewise the third year. The problem is that you never have your IRA money in a consolidated mass that you can invest for capital efficiency. You've created separate plates of investment, and each plate of capital is at least one year from its nearest neighbor. Here's a visual illustration:

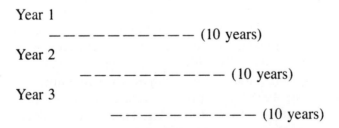

Year 1

— — — — — — — — — — (10 years)

Year 2

— — — — — — — — — — (10 years)

Year 3

— — — — — — — — — — (10 years)

As you can see, you never have more than one matured zero to maneuver. The steplike gradations of sequential plates of zeros don't permit efficiencies of consolidation, which other strategies and other types of zeros do permit. However, if you're an IRA investor who likes the assurance of FDIC or FSLIC backing, likes to invest in an institution represented by mortar and stone rather than by an envelope in the mail, and likes to manage the IRA for convenience, then perhaps the overlapping plate problem won't bother you.

COMMISSIONS AND FEES

Another problem that should bother you is the cost of multiple IRA accounts. There are no limits on the number of IRA accounts you can have, so you can easily have zero CDs alongside CATS in a self-directed IRA alongside a zero bond fund. In theory, the greater the number of alternatives for investment, the greater is your access to zeros for your IRA. In practice, many investors have several IRA accounts so that they can, each year, invest where they find the best zeros.

But also in practice, these same investors pay commissions and maintenance fees as the price for accessibility. Fees for maintenance of IRAs and SERPs are tax-deductible, but over a long period they amount to sizable sums. For instance, most financial institutions will charge $10 to open an IRA and around $25 yearly in maintenance fees. If you have three IRA accounts, figure $75 per year in maintenance fees. That's $1,500 over 20 years. If you'd invested that $75 per year in a passbook account paying 5 percent compounded annually, you'd have almost $2,500 at the end of 20 years. If you'd bought a 20-year zero with that $75 per year, you'd have multiple thousands of dollars as the opportunity cost for the $75 you paid in maintenance fees.

Therefore, just as you learned to be wary of commissions as a detraction from capital and yield, so should you be aware of the costs of maintenance fees in multiple IRAs for which you buy zero coupon investments.

MUNICIPAL ZEROS AS AN ADJUNCT TO IRAs

Municipal zeros shouldn't be held in an IRA or SERP because you'll forfeit their federal tax exemption on municipal interest when you begin receiving payments upon retirement. But municipal zeros can be an excellent supplement to derivative or original issue zeros in retirement anticipation accounts.

We surveyed the advantages of municipal zeros and convertible municipal zeros in Chapters 4 and 5. We saw in Chapter 4 that, on an investment vs. investment basis, municipal zeros outscore zeros in your IRA on several important points, including liquidity, cost, and federally tax-free as opposed to federally tax-deferred returns, although municipal zeros don't provide the tax offsets of IRAs. (Of course, neither will your IRA if you're no longer eligible for deductions.) In Chapter 5 you saw that convertible municipal zeros provide federally untaxed accumulations and federally untaxed current income, neither of which was the case with zeros in the IRA or SERP.

However, the important point is that you don't have to choose municipal zeros over zeros for the IRA; you can have both, mating tax-deferred growth from the IRA with federally untaxed growth and income from municipal zeros. All in all, there can hardly be a more advantageous pairing of investments for future accumulations than by combining municipal zeros with zeros in your IRA or SERP.

There are several ways this can be accomplished, but most investors follow a permutation of the lump sum component of the portfolio discussed in Chapter 11. In other words, they select municipal zeros maturing during periods of professional vulnerability or municipals maturing to coincide with zeros in the IRA. The combination provides a comfortable financial pillow with ample future income.

Although zeros have long been hailed for their advantages in IRAs and SERPs, zeros held outside these retirement anticipation accounts can multiply your wealth exponentially. You need not forsake one aspect of your zero coupon investments for another, and by blending zeros of many types you can achieve comprehensiveness and profits in your investment program.

ZEROS AND THE LAPSED IRA

Post-1986 tax laws may have made you ineligible to deduct your contributions to an IRA. If so, there's little reason to continue making contributions. Not only do you not receive the tax break, but you also have to fill out an additional tax form for nondeductible contributions as well as tolerate the customary penalties for premature withdrawals.

However, you don't want to close your IRA, for amounts presently invested will continue to compound tax-deferred and you'll pay a withdrawal tax penalty unless you're at least age 59-1/2. What you will want to do is assure that the zeros in your IRA produce optimum tax-deferred compounding if you'll not be adding to it.

One way to do that is to invest with the peak of the yield curve. By assembling your zeros and investing them where the economy offers the highest yield elbow, you'll accrue the highest rate the economy is offering at the time. When the zeros mature—or before, if you've received attractive capital gains—you again reinvest at the yield elbow.

For example, in early 1989 the yield curve elbow essentially peaked in 1994. Treasury securities maturing that year provided an 9.2 percent yield to maturity, whereas Treasuries maturing in 2015 and beyond provided less than a 9 percent yield to maturity. Other things being equal, the investor who won't be making further contributions to an IRA would prefer to invest in shorter zeros now and reinvest their matured accumulations later. In this way, the IRA provides continuing investment opportunities without continuing investment.

Invest with the yield curve for sums presently in lapsed IRAs, and invest in municipal zeros instead of your IRA if your account is no longer tax-deductible. Accreted interest from zero municipals is federally untaxed, not merely tax-deferred. Municipal zeros can be sold before maturity without tax penalties, unlike your IRA if you are younger than 59-1/2. They also offer the same advantages of cost, compounding, and predictability that are offered by taxable zeros in your IRA.

SUMMARY

With the exception of zero coupon municipals and EE Savings Bonds, all the zeros you've met are highly useful for your IRA and SERP accounts. With their predictability, convenience, and compound growth, zeros can serve your retirement intentions whether you're retiring next year or in the next century. As you've seen, there are several strategies for managing zeros in your tax-deferred accounts, any of which can produce the returns you need for a dignified and deserved retirement.

With proper attention to quality, maturity, and commissions, your zeros can serve your retirement portfolio as thoroughly as they serve other aspects of your investment program. And finally, even though zeros are best known for their advantages in IRAs and SERPs, zero coupon investments held outside retirement anticipation accounts can provide extraordinary gains for later years.

SPECIAL ADDENDUM TO THE NEW DOW JONES-IRWIN GUIDE TO ZERO COUPON INVESTMENTS: MANAGING ZEROS DURING CHANGING ECONOMIES

The longest economic boom of the postwar era must, like all economic expansions, end. Some authors insist today's expansion will end in the most devastating depression on record, whereas others insist inflation will destroy your portfolio before depression has a chance to do it. Despite their most certain and self-assured forecasts, our economic situation says nothing so certain and assured. For more than a year, we've been seeing economic signals of every kind, and securities markets have alternated between good and bad every month. We have a new president and Congress who have formidable economic challenges ahead of them, and we have a Federal Reserve chairman who is relatively untested in his post.

You enter into this fray with your money and your interest in zeros. You've learned to make the most of zeros in your portfolio, but you can do even better with your knowledge if you understand how economic cycles affect their performance and your incentives to invest. Accordingly, this new edition ends with a discussion of economic cycles and how to manage your zeros during economic change.

ZEROS AND THE "NORMAL" ECONOMY

Cycles of expansion and contraction are normal for our economy, and economic "normalcy" is reflected in a picture you've seen before: a positive yield curve.

FIGURE S–1:
Positive Yield Curve

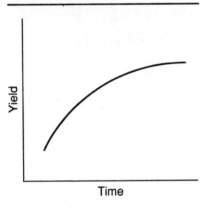

This yield curve and the economy that produced it are said to be normal because interest-bearing securities generally provide highei yields as maturities increase. This picture of an economy with no apparent surprises is the basis for many of the decisions you can make when investing in zero coupon securities during normal times·

As we noted earlier in this hypothetical example, the yield elbow appearing at about 12 years of maturity indicates where the economy is offering its highest yields. There are many reasons why you would select shorter or longer maturities in your personal portfolio decisions; that is to say, you know there are valid reasons why you might not center your purchases of zeros exactly upon the yield elbow years. Perhaps you're filling in the savings component of your portfolio, in which case 12-year maturities are too distant for capital stability. Perhaps you're serializing zeros in your IRA and you want 20-year zeros for your strategy.

In either case, this yield curve and the normal economy it represents don't provide any clear disincentives to any maturity or suggest that you should avoid any one type of zero. Nor, for that matter, is there any indication that the economy is turning against you. In this happy situation, the full range of products and portfolio choices is open to you.

But when economies change, that happy situation changes. Sometimes economic patterns run away with themselves, and normal economic growth becomes unsustainable. Eventually the pattern of normalcy ends, and a new economic pattern asserts itself. Inflation is the first of the "abnormal" economic patterns you might confront as an investor in zeros.

Inflation presents one overwhelming advantage to zero investors: it produces higher yields on new and existing securities. In comparison with your personal rate of inflation and managed consumption, inflated economywide yields can present genuine increases in your returns.

Inflation has one major disadvantage for zero investors: higher yields depress prices of existing zeros. If you are holding zeros and inflation has beaten down their prices, you suffer capital losses if you must sell. But if you understand the progression of inflation, you can diminish capital losses and boost investment yields throughout the inflationary pattern

ZEROS FOR THE ONSET OF INFLATION

During onset of inflation, T-bills and money funds are definitely the zero investment of choice. Other zeros lose price while inflation-generated yields increase. T-bills and money funds increase your yields and retain capital stability throughout an inflationary progression, but particularly at onset, when the sight of inflation makes investors jittery and their concerns make zeros volatile.

With onset of inflation, the longest zeros will take the greatest beating in price. For active managers of portfolios, onset of inflation triggers sales of long zeros, but you don't have to sell just because they do You might be holding zeros for a specific portfolio purpose, such as children's tuition or retirement income. If those zeros are serving their purposes and you're willing to ride out price declines, don't let an economic pattern overrule their place in your holdings

However, during onset of inflation, postpone investing new cash and matured investments in long zeros. Their prices won't have adjusted to higher interest rates, so you lose capital stability and inflation-level rates of interest with premature purchases. Also avoid capital stable but fixed rate zeros like zero CDs and EE Savings Bonds, because their rates won't increase as a maturing inflation produces opportunities for higher rates. Roll matured investments and new capital into T-bills and money funds.

ZEROS FOR FULLY CONFIRMED INFLATION

Within eight months or so after onset, inflation will produce its key characteristic, *negative* term-yield with yield elbow early in term structure.

FIGURE S–2:
Negative Term-Yield

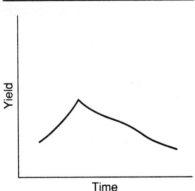

Your best income opportunity from this stage of inflation is to invest in zeros maturing *at the yield elbow,* where term-yield announces highest yields for the confirmed inflation. As inflation matures, term-yield will shift toward a longer maturity. Therefore, short-term zeros maturing at the first yield elbow won't reward your portfolio throughout the inflationary cycle. They will, however, secure market-level returns provided by the first stages of an inflating economy.

ZEROS FOR MATURING AND DECLINING INFLATION

As inflation matures, yields to maturity on zeros approach their highs for the cycle. To estimate the time inflation has matured for its cycle, follow reports of inflation in the press and monitor yields of T-bills and other confirming sources. Investors show greater enthusiasm for locking in rates on longer zeros, and their prices increase. This economic and market evidence tells you that a positive yield curve is beginning to reassert itself. You can recognize this phenomenon by a shift in the yield elbow to a slightly longer maturity and by creation of a second yield elbow at a further point of maturity.

FIGURE S–3:
Camel-Backed Yield Curve
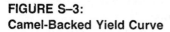

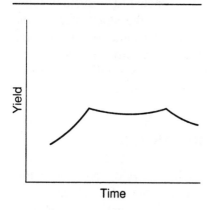

This is the time to move out of T-bills, money funds, and short-term zeros. Invest in maturities between yield elbows and no further than the distant elbow for three reasons. First, zeros formerly at the apex of inflation will now be closer to expiring, so their current yields will be only slightly more attractive than T-bills. Second, T-bill yields will have declined at this stage of inflation. There is yield inducement to go longer. Third, higher yields at the second elbow indicate the economy has not wrung all the inflation out. So, further adjustments in the economy and markets will be necessary before term-yield reasserts a positive slope, and the cautious investor should avoid maturities beyond the distant elbow.

Following this strategy achieves two purposes: you lock in yields to maturity on zeros with prices battered by inflationary interest increases, and you position the portfolio for price appreciation when inflation and its interest rates abate.

For locking in yields, look to corporate, Treasury, and municipal zeros. Zero CDs and many types of zero funds will also be offering their highest yields for the cycle. If you want to hold your zeros to maturity, this will be the most advantageous time to buy, and you may expect to enjoy double-digit yields for decades to come.

These same investments, excluding zero CDs, will also be those that appreciate the most in price as inflationary interest rates increase. Many investors who purchased zeros during the Carter era inflation discovered how handsomely their prices increased when inflation and interest rates fell during the Reagan administration.

Equity investors will be particularly attracted to zero/stock funds at this time. Inflation often is not a friend to the stock market, but its demise is promising for stock prices. By the same token, inflation will have battered the price of zeros in the portfolio, requiring fewer of them to underpin the capital recovery assurances of backstopping the portfolio. The result can be above-average gains.

ZEROS AND BUSINESS CYCLE RECESSION

During the contraction phase of the business cycle, many investors avoid buying corporate zeros, especially those of cyclical industries, because of the declining earnings and business risk associated with recession. Some types of industries often do well during mild recessions. As the number of corporate zeros expands, you may be able to take advantage of zeros from food, beverage, insurance, and other "recession industries" that maintain corporate earnings despite the decline in the economy at large. Look especially to corporate convertible zeros as a chance to participate in stock gains from recession industries.

As a generality, however, the contraction phase is the time to reduce, if not rid, your holdings of corporate zeros. Corporates maximize your exposure to business, market, and economic risks during recession for a whole category of zeros. When the business cycle is down, it's more than logical to remove zeros most affected by the cycle.

One way to step aside from the U.S. business cycle is to buy zeros functioning in a foreign business cycle. Our international neighbors may offer opportunity for sound zeros if they are not sharing U.S. recession. All major brokerages carry mutual funds and unit trusts that hold foreign zeros.

Municipal zeros also provide a means of stepping aside from the business cycle. Municipals have traditionally been highly safe investments; defaults have been rare even in hard times. If you choose municipals in any uncertain economy, it's best to concentrate on general obligations rather than revenue zeros. GOs are backed by the taxing power of the state or municipality, whereas interest payments from revenue zeros depend upon revenues from the project they financed and may be less secure. Wherever possible, seek AAA-rated monies.

TREASURY ZEROS FOR BUSINESS CYCLE RECESSION

There is no more obvious a response to recession than buying Treasury zeros to exempt your portfolio from the business, market, and default risks attendant to recession. U.S. recessions typically last less than two years. Accordingly, one strategy is simply to preserve your capital during recession and await the upswing. You can do this by holding Treasuries of short maturities, and be confident that your income is secure and that your principal will be intact when the expansion starts over.

As always, T-bills and Treasury money funds will preserve your capital during a business cycle recession because they are capital stable. The same is true of zero CDs. Neither, however, will pay attractive yields during a conventional recession. As the heritage of the monetarist school of economics, contemporary theory holds that expansionary Federal Reserve policy of easing interest rates and increasing the money supply will stimulate business investment and

consumer spending to counteract the declining income that character-
izes recession. Expansionary policies will reduce interest rates on T-
bills, CDs, and newly issued zeros of all types.

The advantage of declining interest rates, however, is increases
in prices of existing zeros, especially Treasury zeros. If the recession
is mild and does not damage the municipal sector, existing municipal
zeros will also produce price gains. The investment result is that Treasuries and municipal zeros (as well as funds that contain them) will
produce high-quality accreted interest and capital gains—an exception
to the general rule that zeros are not capital growth investments.

Having selected Treasury and perhaps municipal zeros as
your preferred zeros during business cycle recession, the question
becomes, which maturities are best to take advantage of the growth
that reduced interest rates provide? In general, longer maturities
pick up more in price with interest rate declines. However, business
cycle recession may make investors wary of long-term commitments.
Therefore, an advised strategy is to select zeros with maturities
slightly behind the yield elbow.

FIGURE S–4:
Recessionary Yield Curve

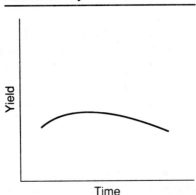

During recession, the yield curve is typically flat and rates are
largely undifferentiated across a long term of distant maturities. Look
for zeros slightly behind the yield elbow, because there is too much
uncertainty associated with longer maturities. Until the course of

recession is more certain and is reflected in term structure, prices and yields behind the elbow might oscillate violently.

The flat yield curve doesn't always appear when the economy is in outright recession. In late 1988, for example, the term structure of interest rates essentially peaked at 8.5 percent yields to maturity for bonds in the early 1990s, ascending to only modestly higher yields for bonds maturing well beyond 2000. Economic news was mixed during that period, but by no means did it confirm the undifferentiated yield curve of recession. Nonetheless, wise investors held their maturities to the area of the yield elbow, awaiting confirmation of behavior for maturities that were much longer.

ZEROS AND INFLATIONARY RECESSION

Inflationary recession—*stagflation*—is characterized by increases in the general price level and interest rates, reductions in employment and industrial production, and intermittent decreases in national income. An inflationary recession, sometimes called a *low growth recession,* is a business cycle whose peak refuses to continue a pattern of growth and also refuses to enter a downturn characteristic of a conventional recession.

Inflationary recession is often a transitional economy that bridges the period between more definitive cycles. However, it can be long

FIGURE S–5:
Stagflation Yield Curve

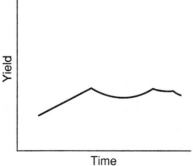

Yield

Time

and pervasive, as was the case with the stagflation of the early 1980s. When inflationary recession persists, term-yield can be surprisingly positive, but highly unstable, for each term of maturity.

The economic combination of stagnating earnings and persistently high interest rates will ravage corporate zeros and corporate zero funds at the onset of inflationary recession. Economywide business risk calls for you to step aside from corporate zeros, and persistently high interest rates call for short-term investments. You attain both objectives at the onset of inflationary recession with short-term Treasury zeros and, especially, T-bills and money funds.

At the onset of stagflation, you can follow these alternatives:

• Hold and buy T-bills. They'll produce market-level yields, preserve capital, and exempt your portfolio from the business cycle run amok.
• Hold and buy short and intermediate Treasury zeros for relative price stability and total returns.

As stagflation persists, a third alternative enables you to enjoy some of the price appreciation and total returns that stagflation produces:

• Start buying back the long-term zeros you sold at the onset of inflationary recession.

As inflationary recession persists, long zero prices will cave in. This produces higher current yields and yields to maturity. Acquire long zeros, preferably Treasuries, for the merit of yield while stagflation persists. When inflationary recession abates and interest rates fall, your zeros will produce capital gains. There's an irony in this third alternative: you don't want to hold long-term zeros during an inflationary recession, but you do want to be buying them so that you can own them when stagflation abates.

ZEROS FOR ECONOMIC DEPRESSION

A depression is *total* and *continuing* macroeconomic decline in a *national* economy's business output, business and personal income, employment, values of corporate and personal assets, consumer confidence, prices, and virtually any economic measure that can be measured. It is business cycle recession at its worst.

You don't buy or hold corporate investments when an economy and business earnings are deteriorating massively. You will hear that blue chip zeros are acceptable during depressions. This may be true following a depression, but when depression hasn't descended to its pits, you simply do not own corporate investments because market, default, and economic risks are too severe. Rid your portfolio of corporate zeros.

When an economy is collapsing, capital stability is a prime attraction in any investment, and T-bills offer it. So do money market funds containing only Treasury and agency securities. Do not expect attractive income returns, however, from T-bills and Treasury money funds. The Federal Reserve's policy of lowering interest rates and expanding the money supply—the doctrinaire monetary policies to combat depression—will not produce higher interest rates on T-bills.

Having read this far, you know that lower interest rates produce capital gains from publicly traded zeros. Knowing this, you might expect Treasury-backed zeros to gain in price during depression as monetary policies take effect. The problem with applying this knowledge in the event of a depression is twofold.

First, the key economic issue of depression is an absence of economywide income. Although zeros can be serialized to produce income, they do not produce continuous income as do coupon-paying Treasuries. Accordingly, conventional income investments would logically be more popular, and there is some question whether investors would buy zeros during a depresssion. Regardless of declining interest rates, zeros must have market demand—investors willing to buy them—in order to produce price gains. Without it, zeros could languish without producing capital gains, a situation contrary to the case of milder recessions.

Second, derivative Treasury zeros of the type we now know as CATS and TIGRs weren't available to investors during the last great depression. For that matter, Savings Bonds weren't issued until 1941. As a result, there's no historical evidence of Treasury zero behavior upon which to base an investment recommendation for a future depression.

You can make more knowledgeable predictions about EE Savings Bonds. It seems highly likely that EEs could be advisable investments during depression, for they'll hold their prices and continue to produce accreted interest. Converting EE to HH bonds will also provide a source of current Treasury income during a depression.

SUMMARY

At onset of inflation, you should secure inflating market-level yields and preserved capital stability with money market funds. As negative term-yield confirms inflation, take cycle-high yields with investments that preserve capital stability while reserving capital for later stages in the cycle. As inflation matures and diminishes, shift your focus to the distant elbow of camel-backed term-yield. Then, when the economy reasserts a positive yield curve, you will be left holding high-yield securities with rates that reward your patience and knowledge of inflation and zeros.

You can wait out business cycle recession with T-bills, Treasury money market funds, and short-term Treasuries. You can also take advantage of countercyclical Federal Reserve policies that loosen the money supply and lower interest rates with Treasury and municipal zeros that mature slightly behind the yield elbow.

Inflationary recession is a particularly difficult economy. T-bills will be uniformly advisable as a buy-and-hold investment, but you can take advantage of battered bond prices if you gradually buy back the zeros you sold at the onset of stagflation. When stagflation remits, you will retain high yields to maturity and secure capital gains.

Depression is the most disastrous of the runaway economies that emerge from a business cycle, and many types of zeros haven't been tested in a depression. But Treasury bills, Treasury money funds, and EE or HH Savings Bonds will preserve your capital by providing assured income and immunity to the treacheries of the economy.

CONCLUSION

As we close, we return to the premise that's guided our discussion, namely, that zero coupon investments have dozens of uses in a contemporary portfolio. Quite apart from their distinctive service in Uniform Gifts to Minors Accounts and Individual Retirement Accounts, zero coupon investments can provide capital stability, current income, capital growth, aggressive gains, and lump sum accumulations for today's investors.

The types of zeros you've studied have ranged from the familiar EE Savings Bond to new zeros like convertible corporates. Whether they've existed for decades or won't come of age for decades more, each zero fits singular functions within each component of the portfolio. Together they consolidate into a cohesive whole. Singly or in combination with other zeros or other types of investments, zero coupon securities serve the portfolio with simplicity and predictability.

The strategies you've examined for managing zeros have originated with knowledgeable investors who looked beyond the conventional and saw how zero coupon investments could be used in ways that their advisors and other investors had neglected. Where others saw only limitations, these investors discovered a pattern, and in maneuvering their zeros into new portfolio territory they created new paths for all of us to follow.

We have yet to see the full impact of zero coupon securities in financial markets and American life. But it is certain that conscientious investors of all ages will be putting zeros to use in new and profitable ways.

Zero coupon investments belong in your portfolio. Even if you don't plan to accrue a million dollars, zeros can assist you in achieving whatever financial objective you've set. Whether your conservative intentions keep you invested strictly in T-bills and money market funds or your gunslinging aggressiveness takes you into long-term zeros purchased on margin, zero coupon investments can reward your investment inclinations.

With the incredible number of zeros available—to say nothing about new zeros that surely will be developed—every investor can be a winner. Now that you've finished *The New Dow Jones-Irwin Guide to Zero Coupon Investments,* all you have to do is put your new knowledge to work in whatever way is most rewarding for you.

APPENDIX

FEDERAL TAX CONSEQUENCES OF ZERO COUPON INVESTMENTS

The tax man defines the difference between purchase price and par value of a zero coupon security as an *original issue discount*. The rest of us call it *accreted interest*. Even though corporate and Treasury zeros realize the full amount of their discount—that is, pay interest—only upon maturity, the IRS usually expects you to pay federal income tax on a portion of the discount each year as if the interest actually were paid. This tax requirement is called *taxation on phantom interest*, and it applies to zeros held outside tax-deferred accounts.

For most zeros, you must calculate each year the interest your zero "paid" even though you won't receive it until the zero matures, is sold, or is called. That is no small problem, and changes in post-1986 tax laws made the problem more difficult. In computing your yearly tax liability on zeros held outside tax-deferred accounts, there are a thousand qualifications. Your zeros will have to be examined on a case-by-case basis depending on whether you bought the zero when it was originally issued or in a secondary market, the date of issue regardless of when you purchased it, whether you inherited it, and the type of zero. Within these ranges, you pay phantom interest tax either yearly or when you dispose of the bond. You will calculate that interest using a straight line constant interest method, or you will use a compound interest calculation as if the zero were a conventional coupon-paying bond.

The Tax Reform Act of 1986 eliminated the tax distinction between interest payments and capital gains. However, future tax laws may reinstate favored capital gains taxation. For this reason you must also be able to distinguish between interest and capital gain. If you sell a zero prior to maturity, you might receive a sales price that is greater than the amount of accreted interest *represented in your sales price*. The difference between interest realized on sale and the amount you received is a capital gain. At present, there's no tax distinction between the sources of gain, but there might be one in the future.

Before we proceed further on this subject, know this: If you're going to buy *any* corporate or Treasury outside a tax-deferred account, you *must* request copies of IRS Publication 1212, "List of Original Issue Discount Obligations," and IRS Publication 550, "Investment Income and Expenses." Both are free for the asking from the IRS.

IRS Publication 1212 will categorize your zero according to year of issue and will direct you as to how to compute the amount of phantom interest on which you must pay tax. In many cases it will specify for you how much tax you owe; in more cases, unfortunately, it merely aids you in working through the computations. Included in Publication 1212 is an exhaustive—but by no means definitive—list of corporate and Treasury zeros (as well as T-bills and government agency zeros) and computed yearly interest liability per $1,000 par value. It is not complete, but it is absolutely indispensable if you're going to invest in federally taxable zeros outside tax-deferred accounts. Publication 550 is a useful cross-reference.

The IRS generally recognizes seven categories of zeros.

Corporate zeros issued after 1954 and before May 28, 1969. This category also includes government obligations issued before July 2, 1982. The investor pays no tax on accreted interest until the year in which the obligation is sold, exchanged, or redeemed. If you sell the zero at a loss, the entire loss is a capital loss and no reporting of accreted interest is required. If you sell the zero at a capital gain, a portion of the return will be taxed as interest income and the remainder will be taxed at capital gains rates. IRS Publication 1212 covers this situation adequately.

Corporate obligations issued after May 27, 1969, but before July 2, 1982. If you bought these zeros *when they were originally issued,* you're in luck because the issuing corporation is obligated to give you a completed IRS Form 1099-OID showing the amount of accreted interest you owe for that tax year. For zeros issued during this period, you're expected to declare phantom interest income each year, but the issuer has to tell you how much. No computations are required on your part.

However, the interest declared on Form 1099-OID applies for you only if you held these zeros for the entire year. If you owned these zeros for less than a year, you have to figure your taxable phantom interest yourself. If you bought zeros issued during this period after they were originally issued—that is, if you bought them in secondary markets—you still receive IRS Form 1099-OID, but it's probably useless. In most cases applying to this situation, IRS Publication 1212 will reveal the amount of phantom interest you must declare.

All zeros issued after July 1, 1982, and before January 1, 1985. If you bought these zeros *when they were originally issued* and held them for the entire year or that part of the year after original issue, you'll again receive Form 1099-OID telling you how much phantom interest to declare.

If you bought these zeros *when they were originally issued* but did not hold them for the full year, divide the original issue discount by 365 and multiply the result by the number of days you held the zeros.

If you bought these zeros *after their original issue,* you'll again receive Form 1099-OID, and again it will probably be useless. If the zero is listed in IRS Publication 1212, you're in luck, because the publication will reveal the amount of taxable phantom interest per bond. If the zero isn't listed in the publication, you have to calculate phantom taxable interest yourself based upon a procedure called *constant interest corresponding to the accrual period.* IRS Publication 1212 provides the procedure.

All zeros issued after July 1, 1982, and purchased before July 18, 1984. If you purchased zeros within this calendar window, you paid more than the bonds' original purchase price plus accreted interest. This *acquisition premium* is essentially a capital gain built into your purchase price (the gain resulted because interest rates fell and prices of zeros increased). You may adjust the base on which phantom interest is calculated by a partial amount of the acquisition premium. IRS Publication 1212 tells how.

All zeros issued after December 31, 1984. Phantom taxable interest on these zeros is taxable yearly as if it were received in semiannual payments like coupon interest formula on conventional bonds. IRS Publication 1212 shows how to compute taxable interest owed for each semiannual accrual period. Each six months that you owned the bond forms the basis upon which you compute phantom taxable interest for the next six-month period. To determine phantom taxable interest for subsequent accrual periods (half years, essentially), you add the result of the first calculation to the purchase price of the bond and repeat steps outlined in the publication.

Stripped bonds and stripped coupons acquired after July 1, 1982, and before January 1, 1985. The procedure for calculating taxable phantom interest for this category of zero is essentially the same as in the preceding paragraph, except the interest method is based upon the number of one-year holding periods or is rateable each day if you didn't own the zero for an exact set of one-year periods. The procedure outlined in IRS Publication 1212 applies to any zero *bought during this calendar window* regardless of when it was issued.

Stripped bonds and stripped coupons acquired after December 31, 1984. The procedure for calculating taxable phantom interest is essentially the same as for stripped zeros referenced in the paragraph immediately above, except the interest method is based upon the number of six-month periods of ownership, again also rateable by number of days if exact six-month periods don't apply to your situation.

FEDERAL TAX CONSEQUENCES OF MUNICIPAL ZEROS

Municipal zeros aren't federally taxable, but you are expected to declare the amount of yearly phantom interest as an informational item on your Federal 1040. That amount is calculated using the same method as for taxable bonds issued after July 1, 1982, and before January 1, 1985.

If you sell your zero before maturity or it is called, you may receive a price higher than the amount of accreted interest to that date. Any excess of price received over the amount of accreted interest is a federally taxable capital gain. Under 1989 tax law, that capital gain is taxed as ordinary income.

STATE TAX FOR MUNICIPAL ZEROS

Zero municipals are exempt from federal tax, and some states don't tax accreted interest on their own bonds or on certain types of issues. If you're a resident of such a state or are holding untaxed issues, you pay no state or federal tax on your zeros. Most states, however, tax accreted interest in one of two ways. First, your state might expect you to declare phantom accreted interest yearly. Second, your state might require you to declare accreted interest when the bond matures or when you sell it.

If your state taxes accreted interest yearly, your state Internal Revenue Service will provide you a formula for determining that interest. Request the formula from your state IRS, or ask your broker for it. Generally, the formula for determining taxable interest in your state will be par value minus purchase price divided by years to maturity. This is the straight line method of calculating phantom taxable interest, and it's in common use for zero coupon municipals.

To illustrate, say you purchased $100,000 of municipal zeros for $10,000 and they mature in 20 years. Your calculation would be

$$\frac{\$100,000 - \$10,000}{20} = \frac{\$90,000}{20} = \$4,500$$

If your state taxes accreted interest yearly according to the straight line method, your state Internal Revenue Service would expect you to declare $4,500 as taxable received interest each year that you owned the zeros. This is also the amount of phantom municipal bond interest that you declare for informational purposes on your Federal 1040 even though the interest is not taxed federally.

If your state taxes the accreted interest when the zeros mature, you would owe state tax on $90,000 of received interest at the end of 20 years. You do not declare this interest received on your Federal 1040 until then.

If your state does not tax interest on this particular zero or on any municipal zero of its own origin, you owe no tax.

CAPITAL GAINS TAX ON MUNICIPAL ZEROS

If you sell zeros before maturity, you may be liable for federal and state capital gains tax (assuming the zero produced a gain) and tax on accreted interest at the date of sale. Typically, capital gains from zeros are defined as sale price minus purchase price minus phantom interest presumed to have been received.

For example, say that you sold the zeros in the example above for $15,000 after owning them for one year. Sale price of $15,000 minus purchase price of $10,000 leaves $5,000. However, when you sell a municipal zero prior to maturity, a portion of the gain is usually presumed to be payment for accreted interest—in this case, $4,500 as determined by the straight line formula. Therefore, your $5,000 total return is $4,500 in interest and $500 in capital gain. The federal government won't tax the interest portion of the total return; your state government may or may not, depending upon whether or not it taxes municipal interest; both will tax the capital gain.

Selling municipal zeros at a loss is a more complicated problem if your state taxes accreted interest. Even though you can declare the loss on your federal tax return, thereby aiding your state and federal tax burden, your state IRS might still expect you to declare phantom interest as if you'd actually received it. The unreceived gain can wipe out the actual loss.

To alter our example slightly, let's say you bought the municipal zeros for $10,000 and sold them a year later for $8,000. You have a capital loss of $2,000. You can declare that loss on your Federal 1040. Because states usually determine taxable income on the basis of a federal tax return, the capital loss can help with your state tax liability. However, if your state taxes accreted interest, you are also expected to declare it as received interest even though it never materialized in your checkbook. In our example, you still have $4,500 of phantom interest to declare, even though you never received it and have no prospect of receiving it.

However, state laws are far from uniform. Under some circumstances—difference in state law, differences in treatment of zeros issued at different times—the capital loss might be a full capital loss without obligation to declare phantom interest. If you're going to sell municipal zeros before maturity, consult qualified tax counsel before executing the transaction.

Of course, your situation is improved if your state doesn't tax municipal interest in general or particular issues of zeros. But most taxpayers will prefer to avoid tax—to say nothing of mathematical—problems by holding municipal zeros to maturity. Before selling any zero coupon investment, whether at a loss or a gain, consult a reputable authority to determine the tax consequences.

TAX CONSEQUENCES OF T-BILLS

Accreted interest paid by Treasury bills is federally taxable in the year that the bill matures. If you buy a T-bill this year and it matures next year, you don't declare phantom interest this year. T-bill interest isn't municipally taxable

TAX CONSEQUENCES OF ZERO COUPON CDs

If a zero CD has a maturity of more than one year, phantom interest is federally and municipally taxable each year. Determine the amount by reviewing the categories above as they pertain to the date you purchased the CD.

SUMMARY

The preceding has been a quick and terribly incomplete recitation of how to compute taxable phantom interest on publicly traded zero coupon securities issued during the specified times. Into this hodgepodge of possibilities, other selected circumstances will enter. For example, some corporate zeros reissued to refinance existing debt might not accrue phantom tax yearly despite their year of issue or of purchase, and in cases of bonds issued before TEFRA laws, you might have a declarable capital loss and declarable interest income simultaneously. By all means, consult the referenced IRS publications when you're completing Form 1040 and Schedule A or B for interest declarations. If that doesn't resolve your situation, go to a tax lawyer.

Because the tax computations are so complicated, many investors restrict their holdings of corporate and Treasury zeros to IRAs and Keoghs, which don't require declaration of phantom income until you begin receiving payments from your account upon retirement or permanent disability. However, if you're willing to do a little paperwork, you can triumph over the tax complexities of zeros and use them effectively outside IRAs and Keoghs

GLOSSARY OF TERMS PERTAINING TO ZERO COUPON INVESTMENTS

accreted interest: The difference between par value of a zero coupon security and your purchase price Also called original issue discount. Yearly accreted interest is the amount earned each year that you hold a zero coupon investment.

basis: The amount of a bond buyer's equity in a zero coupon security. Commonly calculated as purchase price plus interest accrued since purchase

basis points: A relationship between a zero's price and yield subdivided into hundredths. One hundred basis points equals one percent interest yield

BIGS: Bond Income Growth Securities. A convertible zero coupon municipal bond.

broker-maintained market: A market for buying and selling zero coupon securities maintained by the brokerage that created the security.

call date: The date on or after which a zero coupon investment may be redeemed by its issuer.

call features: Many zero coupon investments can be redeemed by their issuers prior to maturity. The bond covenant or prospectus will declare the year in which the bond is callable by the issuer.

call protection: The degree of security that an investor has against a zero coupon investment being redeemed by its issuer. Practically, the number of years between today and the call date

capital debenture: When capitalized, a zero coupon security issued by the Federal National Mortgage Association. Uncapitalized, the term *capi-*

tal debenture refers to any debenture, zero coupon or not, included in a corporation's capital debt.

capital gain: Sale price of a zero coupon security minus accreted phantom interest.

CATS: Certificates of Accrual on Treasury Securities. A zero coupon derivative issued by Salomon Bros.

CID: Compound Interest Bonds. The derivative zeros from Kidder, Peabody.

cliff strategy: A technique for arranging a number of zeros purchased over many years to mature all in the same year.

CMO: Collateralized Mortgage Obligation. A type of zero coupon security issued by mortgage institutions and broken into a zero coupon component called a Z-piece.

convertible zero coupon bond: A zero coupon bond that (a) converts into a current income obligation at some period before maturity, or (b) a corporate zero coupon security that can be exchanged for common or preferred stock of the issuing corporation.

COUGRS: Coupon on Underlying Government Securities. The derivative zeros issued by A. G. Becker Paribas.

default: An issuer's failure to pay accreted interest when a zero coupon issue matures

derivative zeros: Zero coupon bonds created by stripping coupon and principal payments from a U.S. Treasury security.

double dipper zeros: Zero coupon municipal bonds with phantom interest not taxed by the issuing state

ETR: Easy Treasury Growth Receipts. The zero coupon derivative bond issued by Dean Witter.

FIGS: Future Income Growth Securities. A convertible zero coupon municipal bond.

Form 1099-OID: An IRS form listing taxable interest on zero coupon securities. Required to be mailed to some holders of zeros.

GAINS: Growth And Income Securities. A convertible zero coupon municipal bond.

income stream arrangement: A technique of managing zero coupon bonds so that they mature in sequential years, thereby producing current income.

intermediate-term zeros: Those maturing between 5 and 10 years after original issue.

IRS Publication 1212:   The IRS publication that reveals the amount of phantom interest taxable per year on identified issues of zero coupon bonds.

LIMOS: Limited Interest Municipal Obligations. A convertible zero coupon municipal bond.

LIONS: Lehman Investment Opportunity Notes. The zero coupon derivative securities issued by Lehman Brothers.

long-term zeros: Those maturing in more than 10 years.

LYONS: Liquid Yield Option Notes. A zero coupon bond convertible into shares of the issuing corporation. Created by Merrill Lynch.

maturity: The date upon which a zero coupon security produces its full payment of accreted interest.

net asset value: The price paid to purchase, and the price received upon selling, shares in a zero coupon bond fund.

original issue zeros: Zero coupon securities originally issued by a corporation, government, or governmental subdivision as zeros. A zero coupon security not created by severing interest and principal payments from a preexisting bond.

PACS: Principal Appreciation Conversion Securities. A type of convertible municipal zero.

phantom interest: The yearly accreted interest that a zero coupon security is presumed to pay each year you hold it, even though payment of interest isn't made until the zero matures.

public market: The listed exchanges through which zero coupon investments can be purchased and sold.

purchase price: The amount paid to purchase a zero coupon obligation.

put features: Provisions within the covenant of a bond that enable the purchaser to sell the bond back to the issuer after an established date at a specified price, thereby preventing indefinite capital loss to the buyer.

rating: The alphabetical designation attesting to the investment quality of a zero coupon obligation. AAA-rated, AA-rated, A-rated, and BBB-rated issues are said to be "investment grade."

RATS: Registered Certificates of Accrual on Treasury Securities. Another trade name for derivative zeros backed by U.S. Treasury obligations.

short-term zeros: Those maturing within five years.

STRIPS: Separate Trading of Registered Interest and Principal of Securities. A special type of derivative zero made possible by the Treasury Department.

target fund: A mutual fund containing zero coupon bonds that mature in a single year, giving the entire fund a terminal maturity in that year.

tax-exempt securities trust: A vehicle for indirect investment in municipal zeros.

TBR: Treasury Bond Receipts. A derivative zero from E.F. Hutton.

TEDIS: Tax-Exempt Discount Income Securities. A convertible zero coupon municipal bond.

TIGR: Treasury Investment Growth Receipt. A zero coupon derivative bond created by Merrill Lynch.

TINTS: Treasury Interest. The derivative zero issued by Shearson Lehman Brothers.

treasury bills: Obligations issued by the Treasury Department maturing in 13, 26, or 52 weeks.

yield elbow: That point in the term structure of interest rates at which the economy offers its highest yields to maturity on Treasury Securities.

yield to call: The percentage a zero will yield to the date at which it is eligible to be redeemed by its issuer.

yield to maturity: The total percentage a zero will yield if held for its full term of maturity.

zero coupon CD: A certificate of deposit that pays interest only upon maturity.

zero fund: A mutual fund or municipal securities trust that contains zero coupon investments. Investors purchase shares in the mutual fund or units in the municipal securities trust as a means of purchasing zero coupon investments indirectly.

INDEX